The Big Rounds

About the Author

David Lintern is an award-winning photographer and writer, an average mountaineer and a below average runner. He has previously been a cinema projectionist, a sound engineer, a youth music worker and a university lecturer, founded a small refugee charity and worked for the John Muir Trust. After a lifetime spent in cities he now lives in the Cairngorms, writes about the uplands, and guides and teaches outdoor photography. *The Big Rounds* is his first book and his website is **www.davidlintern.com**.

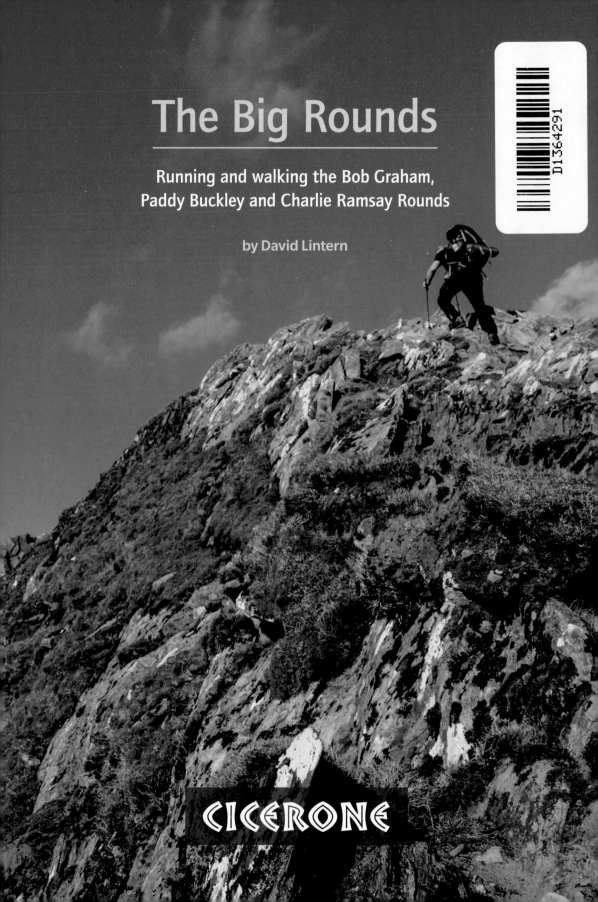

The Big Rounds

Running and walking the Bob Graham,
Paddy Buckley and Charlie Ramsay Rounds

by David Lintern

CICERONE

© David Lintern 2019
First edition 2019
ISBN: 978 1 85284 772 2

Published by Cicerone
Juniper House, Murley Moss, Oxenholme Road, Kendal, Cumbria LA9 7RL
www.cicerone.co.uk

Printed in China on behalf of Latitude Press Ltd.
A catalogue record for this book is available from the British Library.
All photographs are by the author unless otherwise stated.

Route mapping by Lovell Johns www.lovelljohns.com
© Crown copyright 2019 OS PU100012932. NASA relief data courtesy of ESRI

Mountain safety

Every mountain expedition has its dangers, and those described in this guidebook are no exception. All who walk or run in the mountains should recognise this and take responsibility for themselves and their companions along the way. The author and publisher have made every effort to ensure that the information contained in this guide was correct when it went to press, but, except for any liability that cannot be excluded by law, they cannot accept responsibility for any loss, injury or inconvenience sustained by any person using this book.

To call out the Mountain Rescue in the UK, ring 999 or the international emergency number 112: this will connect you via any available network. Once connected to the emergency operator, ask for the police.

Front cover: A runner on the Mamores (Charlie Ramsay Round)
Title page: The climb to Am Bodach (leg 1, Charlie Ramsay Round)

Contents

Looking back over leg 2 from the slopes of Trum y Ddysgi (Paddy Buckley Round)

Dedication

For my kids, your kids and theirs, who will inherit these hills and make their own stories in them.

Acknowledgements

Writing any book is a big deal for the person writing it, and writing my first book about the Big Rounds has been among the harder things I've ever done. While the actual graft was solitary and intimidating, the wider process has thankfully involved dozens of others, without whom the book would not exist.

First, here's to Charlie Ramsay for his positivity and encouragement. Without meeting him, I might only have walked Tranter's Round and no further. Charlie's belief that the rounds are for all to enjoy resonated with my own values, and sowed the seed of an idea for what you hold in your hand. Second, to my partner Tanya, for cajoling me to try Charlie's route despite family commitments, and continuing to cajole me over the following five years to write the whole blessed mess up.

A huge thanks to Cicerone, in particular Jonathan and Joe Williams, whose patience knows few bounds. It helps that Joe is a very accomplished distance runner in his own right, but Jonathan also gave this rookie writer a shot, and then tolerated my Olympian levels of procrastination until it was time to begin to reel me in!

I'm indebted to Roger Smith for his forensic eye and attention to detail. Roger is the author of the famous little green book – *42 Peaks: The story of the Bob Graham Round* – and club member 117, so it was a genuine honour to have him check over the early drafts.

Plainly, this book would be nothing without the hill running community that inspired it. That community is the lion's share of what makes the Rounds unique. Thanks in particular are due to Rob Bushby, Sue Walsh and Jasmin Paris for allowing me to share their Round accounts, and to Paddy Buckley for a glimpse into a lifetime in love with his own wild places. Part of his account of how the Welsh Classical came to be is also included here with his permission.

My thanks also to interviewees Nicky Spinks, Helene Whitaker, Jasmin Paris, Keri Wallace, Wendy Dodds, Jim Mann and Mike Hartell for their generous insights and undoubted achievements, as well as Morgan Williams, Selwyn Wright and John Brockbank for their wise words and advice early on, and Martin Stone and Jon Gay for their open and honest reflections.

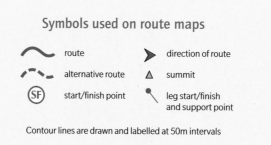

Symbols used on route maps

~ route

▷ direction of route

alternative route

△ summit

(SF) start/finish point

leg start/finish and support point

Contour lines are drawn and labelled at 50m intervals

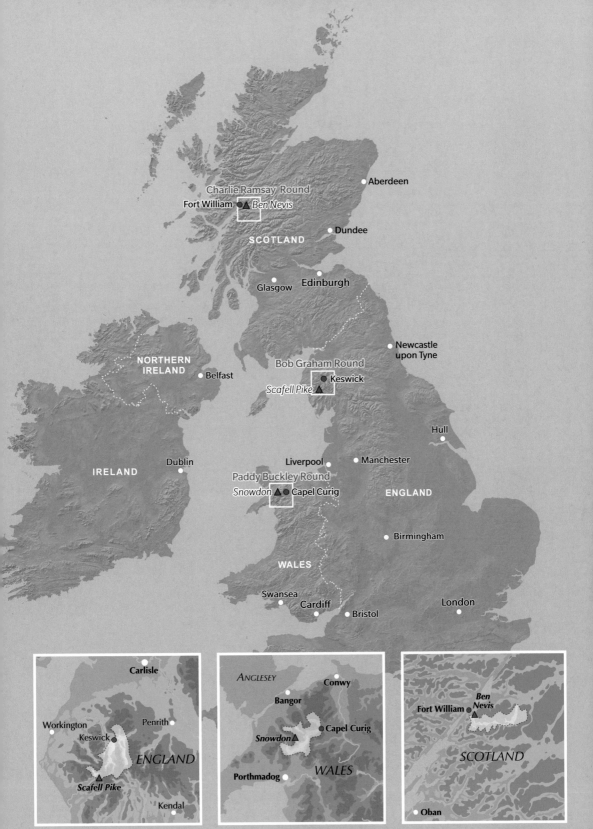

Aberdeen

Charlie Ramsay Round
Fort William ● ▲ *Ben Nevis*

SCOTLAND

Dundee

Glasgow   Edinburgh

Newcastle
upon Tyne

NORTHERN
IRELAND   ● Belfast

Bob Graham Round
Scafell Pike ▲   ● Keswick

Hull

Liverpool   ● Manchester

Dublin ●

IRELAND   Paddy Buckley Round
Snowdon ▲ ● Capel Curig   ENGLAND

Birmingham

WALES

Swansea   London

Cardiff

Bristol

Carlisle

ANGLESEY   **Conwy**

Bangor   **Ben
Nevis**

Workington   Penrith   Fort William ● ▲

Keswick   ● **Capel Curig**

ENGLAND   *Snowdon* ▲   SCOTLAND

WALES

▲
Scafell Pike   **Porthmadog**

Kendal   ● **Oban**

Bob Graham Round   Paddy Buckley Round   Charlie Ramsay Round

An early morning dance with the Devil, on the Devil's Ridge (leg 1, Charlie Ramsay Round)

Preface

Why the Big Rounds?

The hill running community will give you their own answers (some of them in these pages), but these are my own reasons.

I arrived at these rounds, not as a hill runner, but as a means of challenging myself in our island's wild places. Long-distance routes are not the province of hill runners only, and the hills are agnostic – they belong to all of us and none of us, and they don't care if we walk, run or crawl. Passion and persistence are what counts, and they aren't exclusive qualities. But all these statements are generalised, almost to the point of cliché. Why the Big Rounds, specifically?

It's no accident that each of the three includes the highest mountain in Scotland, Wales and England – the Rounds are 'big' in height and well as distance. But it's more than just number crunching that makes these routes appealing. Scafell Pike, Snowdon or the Ben may grab your interest initially, but these ambitious, circular rounds provide an unparalleled sense of journey. Each round is a grand tour on which you get far more than you bargained for.

The beauty of the rounds in my view is not just the tops themselves, but the places in between. For the experienced English, Welsh or Scottish hillgoer on home ground, they are an invitation to get to know familiar landscapes better in a continuous line. In my own personal conversation with these places, the Paddy Buckley in particular was a revelation. I thought I knew most of the ground well enough already, but it turns out I had no idea. I (literally) discovered new sides, faces or aspects to old friends, reached by tiny trods alongside rivers, through woods and over bwlchs (passes). Paddy puts it best: 'I'm delighted when people write to me to say that the Round helped them to make new discoveries – "marvellous country", they say.'

Similarly, the Bob Graham resulted in a more holistic understanding of the entire region, which had previously been abstracted by road travel between discrete areas. The rounds are a perfect way to revisit the familiar as well as discover the unknown. Only the Scottish round was fairly new ground for me at the time, my first experience of one of the Big Rounds in one big greedy gulp, and therefore still my own personal favourite...very closely followed by the Welsh round.

What else? For UK hillgoers in general and the international visitor in particular, the Rounds are a unique opportunity to discover more about our island's peculiar variant of hill culture, and specifically, our unique mountain running culture. The Rounds are made as much of people and history as they are of mountains, and are a great example of how people and place come together, a modern, physical link between us and the land.

Over time, the Rounds have attracted runners from across our island nation (and now the world) to try their luck and test their mettle, and the sport of hill running retains a strong sense of community which sets it apart. Reconnoitring and pacing has forged friendships and competitive spirit across class, region and nation, as each person pushes their personal limit. Indeed, runners will help others to beat their own times, one challenge leading to the next. This camaraderie is something we return to throughout the book. It's not just why the Rounds are so special – it's the reason they exist at all.

For some, a 'Triple Crown' is the obvious ultimate goal. Charlie Ramsay said: 'I think today with the three rounds being unofficially linked as the Big Three, it keeps the challenges alive. The bigger challenge is to do all three, but there's less than 50 people who've done that.'

In addition, all three rounds pass through mountain towns and villages, and there are opportunities to engage with other hill folk (whatever their mode of conveyance). The towns of Llanberis, Fort William, Keswick and smaller settlements on or near the route still retain their

**The Great Gable Memorial
(leg 4, Bob Graham Round)**

own sense of place, something harder to find in many of our larger conurbations, and that's to be celebrated.

That sense of place is carried into the hills themselves. Mountain light can be hard and high contrast, or milky soft, and all the rounds face the sea and share a Celtic gentleness, but even so, for me each round has its own particular colour temperature. If Lochaber is pink, then Cumbria is blue and Snowdonia is gold. If this sounds absurdly romantic, then I plead guilty... just wait until you are on your first top for sunrise!

Before I get too carried away, the scale of these rounds is significant in the opposite direction, too. The Big Rounds are just that – big – but perhaps not so big as to be inconceivable. For runners, the ultimate challenge may be to get around in 24 hours or less, but for experienced backpackers they offer just the right amount of distance and ascent for a demanding week's walking holiday, with perhaps enough time for transport at either end. For those attempting them as a walk start to finish, the routes are all circular, which means that transport logistics are kept to a minimum and there are no time-consuming shuttles to worry about. So, the challenge is very real, but conveniently shaped and sized.

As such, they are a motivation to mountain lovers of all stripes. Talking to Nicky Spinks for this book, she tells how completing the Bob Graham was a key target for her, even before she had a running career. Success takes time and commitment, but is achievable. Nicky's came after only four years. It seems incredible to me that Jasmin Paris can achieve under 17 hours on a round (the Ramsay) that still takes me days to backpack, but then again, when I started this project, I didn't hill run at all. That's changed, and while I'm certainly not in the same league as any that feature here, I now enjoy running in my home mountains.

So, the rounds have changed me, and whether you are on the clock or not, I can pretty much guarantee they will change you, too. Whether it's how you engage with our wider landscapes, how you engage with your own outdoors practice or some of both...whether you go fast or slow, in whole or in part, all of the Big Rounds are genuine adventures to aspire to, and singular journeys to revel in.

David Lintern

Snowdon from the Moelwynion (leg 1, Paddy Buckley Round)

The stalker's path to Sgùrr Èilde Mòr, leg 1 of the Ramsay Round

Introduction

What are the Big Rounds?

The Big Rounds – the Bob Graham Round, the Paddy Buckley Round and the Charlie Ramsay Round – are known to mountain runners as three of the most difficult 24-hour challenges in the world. Each round is a long-distance classic in its own right, rich in the history and culture of fell or hill running. Thankfully for walkers, they also make magnificent day and multi-day excursions deep into some of the most remote, exciting and beautiful country the UK has to offer.

Collectively, the 'Big 3' take in 113 mountain summits (including the highest peaks in England, Wales and Scotland), more than 25,000m (83,000 feet) of ascent and nearly 300km (183 miles) across three of Britain's most distinct mountain ranges – the Snowdonia National Park in Wales, the Lake District National Park in England, and a vast area of Lochaber in the highlands of Scotland.

Using this book

Unsurprisingly, the book is divided into three main sections, one for each Round. Each of these includes the route notes for the entire Round plus guidance and rules, for those on the clock – which vary from round to round – as well as supplementary logistical information for both runners and walkers. There's also a history of each round itself and an individual runner's account of their long day on the hill.

The book is ordered according to overall difficulty – but not necessarily difficulty for runners! This is a book for all hillgoers, and each reader's mileage will vary. The Bob Graham is the mother of these rounds, and is considered the easiest of the three, and therefore comes first, although 'easy' used in this book is a relative term. The Paddy Buckley is often considered by runners to be the most difficult, but as mentioned elsewhere, it has less ascent than the Ramsay and is not quite as remote. The extra logistics involved for the Ramsay; travelling to reconnoitre, organise support teams at off-road changeover points for a timed attempt, plus the additional weather challenges in Scotland, means that for this book, Charlie Ramsay's Round comes last.

In addition to those main sections, this chapter includes practical information on how to approach the Rounds from a practical, ethical, environmental and safety point of view.

The People of the Rounds chapter gives voice to some of the people who have made these rounds so special. Most of those interviewed have an intimate knowledge of every round, not just one or two. As a result, there are lots of useful tips and comparisons (though no secret trods or shortcuts!). In a book like this, there will always be some woeful omissions, for which I offer my sincere apologies: there simply wasn't room for many I would have loved to include.

Please note that any times, distances and elevations listed are approximate, not exact. Also note that the term 'fell' is used interchangeably with 'hill', especially in relation to the Bob Graham Round.

> *"On the day that a runner attempts their 24-hour round, everything must hang in the balance"*
>
> John Brockbank, fell runner

The book's approach

Part of the magic of the Big Rounds is that the routes are not fixed. While the rules for what constitutes a successful round differ, all offer a list of hills only, and no set way to move between them. Moreover, there is a tradition in hill running of not prescribing an exact line, but of developing the hill craft, route finding and fitness required through repeated reconnoitres. Contenders become finishers and on the way, they are pacers and supporters for others, and have their own 'secret' lines squirreled away to shave seconds off here and there. In that sense, everyone's round is different.

I have tried to ensure that this book stays true to that ethos, and so the written guidance offered here, while precise, is intended 'in the spirit of', or 'inspired by' the Big Rounds. The mapping offers an overview only, and the language of the route guides is I hope open-ended enough to encourage further exploration and investigation.

I have deliberately offered options for both runners and walkers. For those uncomfortable with the inclusion of the latter in a book about what are now seen as predominantly running challenges, a reminder of some of the roots of those routes: Billy Bland, the holder of the Bob Graham record for 36 years (until Kilian Jornet took the record in 2018), returned six years after his astonishing round of 13:53 to do the round again as a steady walk. He completed it in 21 hours. Paddy Buckley points out in The history of the Round that the origins of big days out in the Welsh hills lie in the stravaiging exploits of the Rucksack Club, and Charlie Ramsay reminds us that among his running club, the round he famously extended was known as Tranter's Walk.

My contention is that any hard lines dividing walking and running are a relatively modern notion, and have more to do with commerce and marketing than what goes on when people really start to find their feet in the mountains. That said, there are two reasons why I've sometimes made a distinction between the two methods of travel:

- **Practical** – some lines more commonly used by runners are less optimal if carrying a weighted backpack.

- **Environmental** – some of the regular lines taken by runners are showing signs of erosion, and would be susceptible to greater damage with more, regular footfall. There are instances where this is not desirable or sustainable. There are other instances where deviation from the line would break the flow of the round. I've attempted to interpret this in sympathy with both the landscape and our impact, as well as the sense of each round as a whole. There are some instances – I'm thinking of Yewbarrow in particular – where this is a very difficult call.

I've also resisted the obvious temptation to provide split times or example schedules for runners here, restricting my guidance to a very approximate itinerary for a multi-day push, on the basis that a little knowledge is a dangerous thing and another person's map is not your territory. Use the book to help you and do the work yourself, and the Rounds will reward your efforts a hundred-fold.

In these ways, the route descriptions here are intended to be a start point, not an end point. Please have no doubt that these routes are demanding high-level undertakings, even for so-called 'plodders' with six days food and shelter. I've tried to ensure they remain real challenges for fit and experienced outdoors people.

Mountaincraft and personal safety

These are not mountain routes to begin your mountain apprenticeship on; they are routes that challenge and inspire some of the most experienced hillgoers in the world. What factors should you consider when looking at one of the Big Rounds?

Weather

British mountain weather is notoriously change-able, and these are all Atlantic-facing, westerly mountain ranges. The British climate is officially classed as temperate, but our humidity is very high. In real terms and for visitors especially, that translates as cold and damp! If you are not used

"Mountaincraft is the knowledge and skills to look after yourself safely in the mountains. That includes clothing and other kit, food, navigation and awareness of your own limitations."

Wendy Dodds, fell runner

to our climate, do not get used to it by taking on one of these rounds in one go. You will need to have practised methods of staying warm when wet, sometimes when soaked through. Some of this is achieved through acclimatisation over many years, some through technique and equipment choice.

Scottish weather can be particularly capricious. There is often snow on high ground until late May – and on Ben Nevis there can be snow at any time of year. For all the Rounds, high winds and rainfall mean that hypothermia is a very real risk, especially for runners dressed expecting to move at speed. Ask yourself: what would happen if I was injured and needed to keep warm? Equip yourself accordingly.

Runners attempting a timed challenge will often wait for a 'weather window', but foreign visitors, backpackers and other hillgoers may not have that luxury. There is an account by Keri Wallace in the People of the Rounds chapter, which is worth reading in relation to this plan-ning issue.

A spring snowstorm, looking north from Beinn na Lap (leg 2, Charlie Ramsay Round)

On a related note, all three Rounds entail you spending considerable time exposed and high in the mountains. The routes often enchain a number of summits without losing too much relative height. Escape options are limited, and so thorough planning is essential.

Navigation

Part of the attraction of the UK mountains, and in particular those of Wales and Scotland, is the lack of infrastructure. This extends to signage. The Big Rounds are all unmarked routes. Do not expect to find flags, or 'flashes' to guide you. There may be cairns (piles of stones) and the odd flag, but these may not be relevant to the route you are following, and there are no flashes that relate to these rounds at all. You may encounter an occasional sign at a road or track head, and these are usually remarked upon in the route notes. However, these are the exception, not the norm.

Note that the Bob Graham Club has explicitly prohibited the marking of the Bob Graham Round. It should go without saying that it goes against the ethics of all three rounds to pre-mark or leave a trace in order to aid your own attempt.

As a result, you will be 100% self-reliant on navigation using a map (paper and/or digital) and compass, plus the guidance notes herein. I have deliberately not supplied a GPX download, and the maps contained within are overview maps only. Your navigation skills should include taking accurate bearings, timing and pacing at a minimum. Please ensure you are fluent in these skills. If you cannot navigate competently in all weathers, you run the risk of injury or death.

Mapping

I use and recommend the Harvey Ultra Distance Challenge series of maps for each of the Three Rounds. These are water resistant, at a scale of 1:40,000, or 2.5cm to 1km, and fit the entire route on only one sheet in each case. They also show the suggested changeover points and a few notes from runners or founders. These maps are sometimes referred to in the guidance notes for each round, as is the Ordnance Survey equivalent... especially when there is a discrepancy between the two!

It's also worth knowing that there are some spelling differences in hills and other features between the Harvey and OS. I've mostly gone with the OS versions, but for Scotland referred to Peter Drummond's excellent reference book *Scottish Hill and Mountain Names*.

Fitness

All hillgoers will need a high level of fitness to complete the Rounds, especially in one go.

For walkers, regular outdoor exercise in the mountains on at least a monthly basis, with some recent previous experience of multi-day pushes enchaining multiple hills should ensure a reasonable chance of getting around within a week or less. Other exercise – cycling, running and swimming – will all help to reduce the sufferance quota involved in dragging a pack full of food and camping kit around in the mountains!

Clearly, the requirement for those running a timed attempt is greater, and training over years rather than months is needed. Training falls outside the remit of this book, but it should be obvious that running over rough ground and practising both climbing and descent is of more use than road running. That said, anything is better than nothing, and regular running wherever you are is essential. Hill reps are great at building up leg strength, and both long fell races and pacing others on their round attempts will extend your own stamina and give you the experience to go for a sub 24-hour attempt.

Experience

The best safety precaution you can take is to be fully competent in navigation and self-care in what are potentially hostile mountain environments. This is achieved over years of practice in all conditions and a variety of terrain. It is not learnt from books like this one, videos or even courses. Those things are just the beginning.

There is plenty of good advice in People of the Rounds on building the experience needed for runners. If you are running on the clock, reconnoitre the routes until you are satisfied that you know the way, and have experienced fellow runners with you, but do not rely on them 'dragging you round'.

'You don't get this in the bloody Olympics!' Recce'ing leg 2 of the Paddy Buckley Round

For walkers and backpackers, please note that these routes taken in one go are a stretch – even for the experienced. At the bare minimum, you should have several consecutive years of mountain experience, both summer and winter, in each of the three regions described, before you take on one of the rounds in one go.

All hillgoers should be well prepared and supplied, and have a plan of escape should the weather turn or personal circumstances change.

Last resort

There is a long tradition of self-reliance and self-sufficiency in our mountain culture. This is part and parcel of what makes the Rounds such a unique experience – perhaps even more so for newcomers. Therefore, assume that you will have to self-rescue, and plan and travel accordingly.

Mountain Rescue in the UK hills is undertaken by volunteers (albeit working at a high level of professionalism) who, without payment, help save lives while risking their own. They are organised and assisted by the Police.

Before you go – register your phone with emergency SMS, and understand how this system works (www.emergencysms.org.uk/registering_your_mobile_phone.php).

> **During your challenge** – if you or a companion is injured, cannot move and you need to call for help, call 999 and ask for Police, then Mountain Rescue.
>
> Then, give the following details:
>
> - Location (with a grid reference if possible)
> - Name, gender and age of the casualty
> - Nature of injuries or emergency
> - The number of people in the group
> - Your mobile phone number
>
> Then, stay where you are until you are found.

When to go

The months of May, June and July are most often chosen for a first attempt, since they provide the longest hours of daylight and some of the best opportunities for settled weather. Especially for those attempting a timed challenge, attention should be paid to moon phases – a full moon will aid travel on the night section. For walkers, there is something to be said for September too, when conditions can be settled, but beware that nightfall comes quickly in the autumn, especially in the north of the country.

Winter rounds are different, and weather and snow conditions and related safety matters become even more important, especially since most of the timed attempt will take place in the dark. More discussion around winter attempts can be found in People of the Rounds.

Who to go with

For all three Rounds, if you are attempting the timed challenge it's recommended that you travel with other runners, which increases the margins of safety and your chances of getting round in the time available. It is also more fun, and will help with morale.

To register for a Bob Graham Round attempt, it's not only a recommendation but a requirement that pacers should accompany you, acting both as a safety net and as witnesses to your attempt.

There's more about pacing and support in each specific chapter.

For those attempting the Rounds as a continuous walk, there are no requirements relating to solo travel, but all hillgoers should know their limits and plan and travel accordingly.

Equipping for the Rounds

For runners, shoes that you know and trust, a lightweight running pack, food and a water bottle, and perhaps gels if you use them, are essential. Clothing should match conditions, but be prepared for the worst (for example an unplanned stop high on the mountain). Footwear and clothing changes should be factored in at each crossover point, as well as sustenance. This all takes time to work out and become proficient at.

For those attempting the Rounds as multi-day backpacks, there are specific challenges. As walkers carry more than runners, and take longer, weather and food play an equal but very different role in their Round attempt. They sometimes also travel solo, and navigation is often 'on sight' and without prior reconnoitring. However, walkers

The view from Sgòr an Lubhair (Charlie Ramsay Round)

Winter on the Easians (leg 3, Charlie Ramsay Round)

can learn a lot from the fleet of foot. Faster and lighter is key to the Rounds, even over multiple days. Here are a few tips:

- Get comfortable with wearing unlined trail shoes and practise a 'wet shoe system'. Since you are staying out overnight, keep a second pair of dry socks and a third pair of waterproof oversocks for camp. It does help to be lighter on your feet when covering most of the ground described here, but wearing trail shoes can take a few years to get used to, and you will need to strengthen your ankles and calves. Lined footwear can lead to moisture becoming trapped inside your shoe, and that leads to blisters.

- Your camping kit should be durable and you should be very familiar with it. There will be times where you need to camp high on the hill, and your shelter should be weather tested and highly wind resistant. A tarp and/or bivi bag can be useful to save weight, instead of a full tent with inner, but whatever you use make sure you are warm and comfortable in the evenings. A mixed tent peg set can be useful for a variety of pitching conditions, from rocky, boggy to very windy.

- Our island's wildlife is generally non-hazardous to human life, but camping in the summer necessitates dealing with midges – very small, flying and biting insects. They are not poisonous, but can be a real irritant, especially in sheltered or damp places, so a repellent and a head net are required for a decent rest. If you are bringing a shelter from another country, note that the mesh that prevents harassment by sand and black fly is not fine enough to exclude the much smaller British midge. Clegs, or horseflies can also be an issue – again, these are not poisonous, but they will draw blood.

- Your stove system should be tried and true (fuel can be purchased from outdoor gear shops near the start of each Round), and you should have a set of dry, warm clothes to change into at the end of the day. Drybags are essential for both storage and for maintaining comfort and safety in the British mountains. As well as your navigation tools, you will need a headtorch, a first aid kit and the ability to use it effectively. The UK weather means you should plan for a bit of everything; that means suncream as well as full waterproofs! A windshirt can be a very useful item for both walkers and runners.

- Pack light and only bring what you need. Redundancy is a fine art; knowing what to take and what to leave behind also takes years of practice, and it's vital to practise in the areas that the Rounds cover, not just the hills nearest you. For example, the 'right' amount of warm clothing in the evening will not be the same on the South Downs as it is in Highland Lochaber, and will vary from person to person and month to month.

- Food is difficult to plan for everyone, and what needs to be carried in one go varies from Round to Round, as there are different opportunities for resupply. I have included information about where it's possible to resupply if you are walking, in the guidance notes of each Round. What is true of all three routes is that the days are strenuous, and a balance will need to be struck between carrying enough food to sustain you to the next leg and carrying so much that your onward progress will be too slow! Again, practice over many years makes (nearly) perfect. Take what you know sustains you on a multi-day walk, plus a little more, since these are tough routes. By the same token, you can also expect to lose some weight and be a little hungry at times, but don't cut it too fine: 'Safety first' also includes food.

Environmental impact and leave no trace

There is no excuse whatsoever for littering wild places. That includes **all** food and drink wrappers and containers, including gels. Runners are not exempt.

This also includes going to the toilet in the hills. In some places, especially on the Welsh and English Rounds, groundwater has been contaminated by bad practice in this regard. I've included a section on water in each specific chapter, pointing out where there might be higher risk of polluted water.

Replenishing calories on a backpack of the Ramsay Round

Camping under Great Dodd, on the Bob Graham Round

The solution is to carry a trowel (or use a tent peg or walking pole) to dig a deep hole at least 75m away from running water, then do your worst and completely bury it. Plan ahead, and don't get caught short. Remove all toilet paper and carry it out in a bespoke bag or container. Burning it with a lighter rarely works in our windy, rainy weather, and if it's dry enough to burn, you might start a ground fire and you are dehydrated! If you make use of the bothies on the Scottish Round, a spade and instructions are usually provided. Use both.

When cleaning cups, pans or yourself, do not wash directly in running water, as others may need to drink from the source further downstream. Wash away from the stream or river and dispose of the grey water away from the source. Use organic and biodegradable soaps and toothpaste (or just plain water). Avoid overcooking, and if you do have waste food at the end of a meal, pack all of it out with you in a rubbish sack or ziplock bag.

Camp on durable, well-drained ground and avoid commonly used campsite areas. Any stones removed to erect a shelter should be replaced when you leave. When you leave, there should be zero trace of you having stayed overnight.

The increased popularity of trail running in particular, and walking and hiking in general, has led to erosion in some places on the Rounds. We can all help to mitigate some of this damage by wearing lighter footwear, carrying only the right amount of kit and not over-reconnoitring. As I explain under The book's approach, in certain places environmental conditions underfoot have informed my route recommendations. It is not for me to police the outdoors community, although there are places where I feel we need to use alternate ways around, to let the ground heal again. I've tried to be as transparent as possible about that in this book.

There is plenty of information online on leave no trace principles as they apply in the UK. Please take this as seriously as you plan the rest of your trip; other peoples' challenge and enjoyment is every bit as important as yours.

Access and the right to roam – differences in law and in practice

The right to access the places described in this book is not the same across all three Rounds. The law varies in both principle and practice, in England, Wales and Scotland.

England and Wales

In 2000, the Countryside and Rights of Way (CRoW) Act gave people the freedom to roam across 'open access' land – mountain, moor, heaths, downs and common land – using non-motorised or self-propelled means. You can also access private land if you have the landowner's permission, or if there is a local tradition of access on that land.

Some parts of the routes described in this book make use of paths or public rights of way. Most, but not all, of the moor and mountain land described here is open access. Some of the low-land, farmland and town land, however, is neither. Please take extra care when entering and leaving the glens and valleys for the fells.

Except for the odd exception, the right to stay overnight is not granted in the CRoW Act, and many landowners will understandably prefer it if you do not wild camp in their backyard. You are required by law to ask permission from the landowner to camp, although in many cases this is not practical. Remember that landowners do have the right to move you on if they wish to.

Scotland

The Land Reform Act 2003 gives those in Scotland similar roaming rights to those enjoyed further south, although in practice long established traditions of *stravaiging* (a Scots word, loosely translated as 'strolling' or 'wandering aimlessly') across the land mean that much of the country is regarded as open access even when it is privately owned!

In Scotland, access rights also extend to wild camping, providing you abide by the Scottish Outdoor Access Code (SOAC). Some of this code is covered in the section above on environmental impact, but other best practice includes: avoid camping near houses, farms, roads or historic structures, and do not disturb wildlife or deer stalking.

Heather in bloom on leg 2 of the Paddy Buckley Round

A runner on the Mamores (Charlie Ramsay Round)

In practice

Exercise common sense and decency, and you are fully within your rights to camp informally north of the Scottish border. In the Lake District, a little more discretion is advised, but wild camping overnight on the open fell above about 600m, outside any livestock enclosures and out of sight of roads and houses, is usually regarded as acceptable. In Wales, some landowners have traditionally been a little more territorial. Tucking yourself well out of sight can be a good idea, especially because the Paddy Buckley Round lends itself more to day-sized sections and you may end up in the valley at nightfall.

Be courteous and polite, arrive late to your campsite and leave early, make no noise and leave no trace, and it's highly unlikely that you'll encounter any problems.

There are, however, specific access hotspots on each Round that I have highlighted in the route notes, and mitigating your impact in these places should be taken very seriously indeed. If those of us on the Rounds are irresponsible or rude, leave litter or disturb walls, fences or livestock, we run the risk of upsetting landowners, farmers, residents and the authorities, which might one day threaten the existence of the Rounds altogether.

Please enjoy the Rounds responsibly and leave them as you found them – wild and free. We are

just passing through – others live and have livelihoods to maintain in these places.

The Bob Graham Club sums this up very effectively on its website:

- Respect the route.
- Respect those who live and work along the route.
- Respect the history, traditions and ethos of the Round.
- Don't mess things up for others.

This is (un)remarkably similar to the SOAC:

- Respect the interests of other people.
- Care for the environment.
- Take responsibility for your own actions.

For those using the bothies in Scotland, please note that the bothy code (https://www.mountainbothies.org.uk/bothies/using-a-bothy/) prohibits the use of these unmanned shelters for runner transition or support points, although they could arguably still be used to house members of those teams either before or after a changeover has been dealt with elsewhere.

Black Crag and Pillar (right) from Steeple (leg 4, Bob Graham Round)

The Bob Graham Round

26,778FT (8160M) OF ASCENT OVER 61.4 MILES (98.8KM) AND 42 TOPS

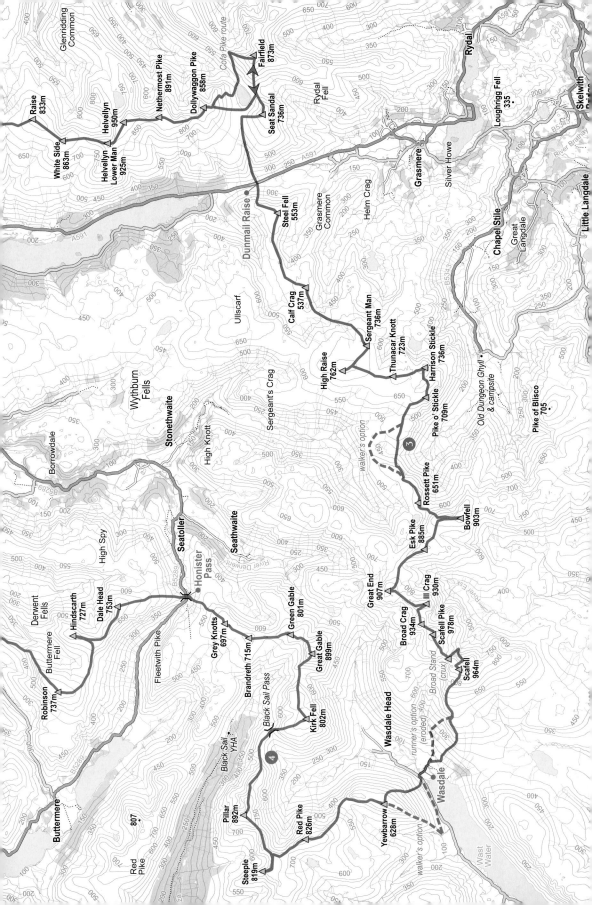

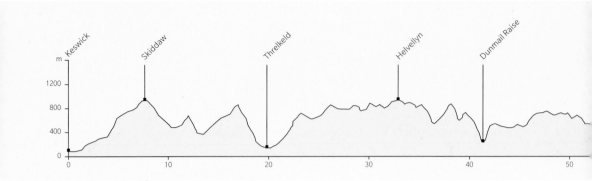

A distant Ennerdale water, from Pillar (leg 4)

The Bob Graham Round is the granddaddy of ultra-distance mountain routes, arguably the first of its kind in the world. It's a roughly circular tour of the Lake District over 61 miles and 42 summits, including the highest mountain in England – Scafell Pike. It has the least amount of ascent of the three rounds covered in this book, but is not the shortest – in fact, it's longer than the Scottish round and shorter than the Welsh one.

It is inextricably linked with the sport of fell running; long mountain challenges that test fitness, navigation and resolve. For many runners it's almost a pilgrimage, inspiring loyalty, love and awe in equal measure. Arguably, travelling on the Bob Graham Round is as much a homage to the history and traditions of the sport as it is about the world-famous scenery.

The round sits entirely within the Lake District National Park in Cumbria, which includes all of England's mountains over 3000ft. It's the busiest park in the UK – as a visitor to the Round you will share the hills (or 'fells') and valleys with around 15.8 million visitors annually. The park was designated a UNESCO world heritage site in 2017, as much for its cultural history as its landscape value.

The landscape has been transformed over millennia by farming and in particular grazing, and from at least the Victorian period onwards, by tourism. For the most part on the Round the area's

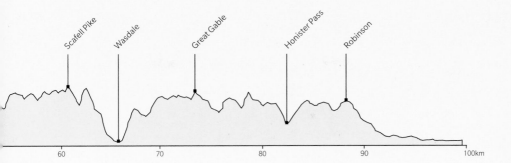

mining history is not obvious – except when you drop into the huge slate quarry at Honister Pass.

It's a volcanic, glaciated landscape and many of the valleys bear a distinctive U shape as a result, often with deep lakes at their centre. On the round itself, you'll see this most noticeably at Wasdale. Geologically, the whole area sits on top of a granite batholith – originally a buoyant mass of magma that pushed the surrounding rock upwards, before cooling and slowing. The north of the round is predominantly sedimentary rock – called Skiddaw Slate locally – subsequent erosion leading to a more eroded, rounded topography. The central and western parts of the Round are a mix of sedimentary and volcanic rock, and as a result the terrain is generally steeper and rougher. Scafell Pike, the highest mountain in England, is the remains of a caldera.

The hills are predominantly bare, but where the sheep are kept in check there is heather moorland and some woodland regeneration. The hedge-rows and associated wildlife in the Newlands valley are a joy to walk or run alongside, and feel quintessentially English.

The Bob Graham Round covers a huge variety of terrain. Legs 1, 2 and 5 going clockwise are gentler and more rolling, while the middle section between Dunmail and Honister (legs 3 and 4) is high, exposed and often loose underfoot. Don't

be fooled by the cosy tourist brochure image of the Lakes – there is plenty of technical ground to cover here.

Whether you are running or walking, you must start and finish at the Moot Hall in Keswick. Clockwise or anticlockwise? Some prefer the latter, to ease themselves in gently on the low ground in the Newlands Valley and the Derwent Fells. Others argue it's good to get the big climbs of Blencathra and Skiddaw out of the way early, leaving easier ground for tired legs at the end. In some ways, it's less critical a decision than on the other rounds in the book, because the toughest terrain is in the middle, whichever way you tackle it. I've chosen to go clockwise, simply because I prefer the rougher terrain of the western fells to the more rolling easterly ones.

The rules for a timed attempt are covered later in this chapter and are very specific, but for those not on the clock, there is nothing to prevent you enjoying the route in whole or in part, with friends or solo, providing you stick to the environmental and ethical guidance outlined in the Introduction. Please be aware that by following in the footsteps of Bob Graham and others, you are also responsi-ble for the ongoing good health and reputation of the Round.

Route Guide

LEG 1

Keswick to Threlkeld

Distance	12.3 miles (19.8km)
Ascent	5272ft (1610m)

This is a shorter stage over two of the biggest hills on the round, which offer superb views and a feeling of space and remoteness, as well as some unforgiving ascent. There's a downhill grade 1 scramble, and a tiring sting in the tail (in the middle of the route).

As with any micro navigation in towns, the beginning of the route can be a little confusing. Once out of town and onto the hill, it becomes more straightforward. Start from the **Moot Hall** in Market Square, at the southern end of Main Street in Keswick. Be mindful of the general public, especially if you're running.

Head downhill (NW) on Main Street, and after a few metres turn right into the ginnel (alley) to the right-hand side of the Golden Lion Pub. Exit the ginnel and go diagonally across the car park, heading for Otley Road, to the left of Keswick Laundry. Once on Otley Road, turn first left then first right to find the path to the footbridge across the **River Greta**. The start of the path has a railing and a green hedge: veer right to go down it.

Skiddaw ridge

Once you've crossed the river, cross Lower Fitz Park, past a BMX track at the edge of the park, following a path to a small metal gate facing an old railway bridge. You can clearly see the break in the railway embankment on the map. Turn right out of the park and onto Brundholm Road. Follow this for approximately 150m and then take the first left on Spoonygreen Lane. You'll join the Cumbria Way and follow this very straight road out of town over the **A66**. As you begin to climb, the road becomes a path and passes through some pretty woodlands.

Contour Latrigg and Mallen Dodd on this easy path to reach an open car park area at NY 280 253. Now follow the path NE and then NNW, contouring around Little Man for your first summit – Skiddaw. The going is fairly steep and sometimes eroded but it's a wide and easily followed path to the top. Head north from the summit cairn for about 600m and then turn east, downhill on short grass to cross a fence. Follow another fence to join the quad tracks through boggy, heathery ground to meet the path to Skiddaw House near a small, old stone bridge over a stream. Note that going by way of Hare Crag is now best avoided due to erosion concerns.

From this bridge, start directly up summit number 2 – Great Calva, heading NE. It's possible to follow a line of shooting butts, if they are visible above the bracken! It's a dull ascent but a characterful, rocky top, slightly marred by a fence divide. From Great Calva, follow this fence and descend south to the second summit, and then turn east. Continue to handrail (follow a linear feature) the fence through bilberry and heather to meet a circular sheep fold (a favourite landmark of Wainwright) in Wiley Gill. Pass this directly on the left, cross over the Cumbria Way briefly and then ford the **River Caldew**. Beware, this can flood. If in spate, head upstream until a fence crosses the river, and use this as a navigation handrail across.

Descending Hall's Fell

You are now at the foot of a long and indistinct climb over **Mungrisdale Common**. It's a dull slog over grass and tussocks, before it eventually flattens out a little to become more mossy and boggy. Head left of the summit screes on the skyline, to reach summit number 3 – Blencathra. The actual summit is slightly beyond the screes, and directly in front of your descent via **Hall's Fell Ridge**.

At the bottom of Hall's Fell, you'll reach a stream; turn right and take the left-hand stile, heading downhill on a bridleway to the farm. Then follow the old sign for the A66 into **Threlkeld**.

SAFETY FIRST

Hall's Fell Ridge is classed as a grade 1 scramble, and is fairly low in that grade, but it does require care especially after the first 200m or so. Those without a head for heights should not attempt these Rounds, and many accidents have occurred on this descent (some involving runners), so if in doubt, go around. There's a very pleasant and sensible descent option to the west, via Knowe Crags and Blease Fell. This leads to the Blencathra centre car park, from which the road east can be taken into Threlkeld.

LEG 2
Threlkeld to Dunmail Raise

Distance	13.4 miles (21.5km)
Ascent	5895ft (1800m)

Going clockwise, a grand but gently undulating ridge enables swift travel, but is not to be underestimated in poor conditions. At Helvellyn, a series of ridges and coves drop away dramatically to the east and the ground underfoot becomes more engaging.

Turn right onto the A66, then take the first left towards Newsham, handrailing a concreted irrigation system on your left. Go through a gate at Newsham House and onto scrubby, then grassy open fell. Runners may choose to approach summit number 4 – Clough Head – directly; make for the edge of the woods on your right, go through a gate and follow a path by a stream to meet the Old Coach Road, before climbing steeply up the north side of **Clough Head**. For walkers, it may make more sense to cut across the open fell SE to intersect Old Coach Road, and then follow it east until you meet an old railway car. Walk on a few metres until approximately NY 340 234, and then ascend on a rough and indistinct path on the spur, avoiding the boggy ground to the east of White Pike.

The going on top is easy and grassy and fantastic views open out towards Great Dodd. My preferred camp for backpacking is nearby. Head towards the characterful **Calfhow Pike** and camp there, or if you need water or shelter, descend SE to cross the beck for some flattish ground at around NY 336 208. Whether you are camping or not, this can be a good place to collect water, as the ridge is mostly dry until Grisedale Tarn.

Calfhow Pike, on the eastern ridge

Helvellyn and White Side, from Raise

Regain the path ESE to summit number 5 – **Great Dodd**. From here, the going is straightforward in good visibility and only Helvellyn makes much of an impression, far in the distance. However, this long eastern ridge of the Round requires very careful navigation if the cloud is down – it's very broad, the hills rise and fall only very gently and there's a good chance of coming off a bearing. On the upside, that means the terrain is easy and the going is fast in good weather.

Descend a path SSW very slightly and regain a slight rise for summit 6 – **Watson's Dodd**. Even in good visibility this seems as if it's a cairn to be bypassed, while looking back from further south it's clear that it's actually a dogleg in the route. On the Bob Graham Round, you must visit it! From Watson's Dodd, head SE and then south to gain another grassy summit (number 7) – **Stybarrow Dodd**. There's a ruined wall here, and a small cairn, but not much else.

Now, go down due south on a clear path towards Stick's Pass, and head on up to the next, and more distinctive rocky summit (8) of **Raise**, with its large cairn finally breaking the grassy monotony. From here, the path stretches out SSW down, and then gently up to meet summit number 9 – **White Side** – with its shelter cairn. A line of cairns marks the path, down and left,

heading south to meet the first of Helvellyn's climbs (**Lower Man**), which actually gets a little more engaging on the ascent as the nose of the ridge narrows.

There's a small col before the final, small pull up to the eleventh summit, **Helvellyn**, with its four-way walled shelter. This is another top to be wary of in bad visibility, as it's rather flat, with some serious drops down to the scrambles of Swirral Edge and Striding Edge on its eastern flank.

Heading south from Helvellyn, a few paths lead off to the west, which bypass the next two hills that we need to visit, so keep close to the ridgeline over rocky and sometimes eroded ground. Descend to the col and then re-ascend a short distance to summit number 12 – **Nethermost Pike**. It's a flat, slabby top and therefore easy to miss the summit cairn (the second one you can see from the main path). The path continues south to another col and then splits on the final ascent. Take the left fork for the actual summit (13) of **Dollywagon Pike**, which has fabulous views of both the route ahead and behind.

From here, runners may wish to descend south following the fence posts, and then do Fairfield out and back from the west end of **Grisedale Tarn**.

My preference is to descend from Dollywagon Pike by the steep, stony switchback path to the

Grisedale Tarn

Grisedale Tarn is a popular and useful place for both camping and hydration, but if contemplating the former, be aware of 'fetch' – the wind picks up over the water and can mean a challenging camp. In calmer weather, there are good pitches to be had at the east end of the Tarn, or if not, some shelter can be found in the shadow of Seat Sandal. You should also consider treating any water you use.

outflow of Grisedale Tarn by the usual walker's route, and head for one of the best little trails in the Lake District.

It runs diagonally ESE, up towards Cofa Pike. It quickly gains height without too much effort. Reach a cairn and turn right for the ridge between Cofa Pike and Fairfield. It is possible, though not necessary, to cut off a little before this, turning south to climb up Fairfield with the occasional use of hands, through blocky slabs on a thinning ridge, until it levels out to the final scree path to the summit (14) of Fairfield. It's an elegant way to

reach this very flat top, which can be disorientating in bad weather. From the tallest cairn, head west to join the eroded motorway of a track down to Grisedale Hause. This is an exposed place and can be difficult in high winds.

From the col at Grisedale Hause, the way onto the next top – Seat Sandal – is obvious. Ascend a rather eroded chute of scree and loose stone until you reach a stone wall. Follow the wall, picking your way through to reach the top. Seat Sandal (summit 15) is a quiet and relatively wild feeling place, benefiting from being in the shadow of more famous neighbours. It has wonderful views to Grasmere.

From the summit, runners may wish to head west, off trail down to the A591 and their support at Dunmail. For others, follow the wall north, steeply down to rejoin the main path exiting from the Grisedale Tarn basin. From here, turn left and head west on a very good and picturesque path which runs alongside Raise Beck down to the road. This invariably takes longer than it should, as the lower section is fairly steep, but it's a classic Lakeland beckside amble and very enjoyable.

At the foot of Raise Beck, find a small stone bridge, a gate and a stile. Cross over the stile and the main road to reach another gate and stile.

A moody Grisdale Tarn

LEG 3

Dunmail Raise to Wasdale

Distance	14.9 miles (24km)
Ascent	6833ft (2080m)

This leg is the crux of the round taken in either direction, over the highest, most exposed ground in England. It is also the longest leg, which for walkers may be better split at Langdale or by a camp on the fell near Angle Tarn. Going clockwise, a stiff climb is followed by a plateau sprinkled with tops that can be tricky to distinguish. After Langdale the going becomes rockier, almost alpine.

From across the road, Steel Fell seems unassailable but on closer inspection there are two gullies. In between them but closer to the left gully, a path leads left from the stile and climbs steeply. Cross the stile and take this for a relatively short, but taxing climb to the top, which is eroded in places.

Once at the top, follow the fence line south, then southwest. This can be followed across a broad plateau of tarns, bog and moss to small cairn at the summit (16) of Steel Fell. Navigation in this area can be tricky in bad weather. From the top, keep the wooden fencing on your right and head WNW, broadly contouring around the head of Greenburn. After around 500m, the fence turns sharply north – ignore this and follow the more distinct path as it turns south, to cross boggy ground and become very intermittent again. Pick your way through rocky outcrops for the final few metres to summit 17 – Calf Crag.

From here, follow a distinct path west, along the ridge overlooking Easedale for a while until it joins the path up from Easedale, at Mere Beck. From here, there is a decision to be made: High Raise or Sergeant Man. My preference is for the latter – it's easier to navigate in bad weather and less steep than heading straight for the former.

Mere Beck is a good water stop, very beautiful and well worth a lunchbreak if you are not on the clock. Climb steeply to the left of this, following the line of old fence posts on a vague path until the terrain levels out, the path becomes more distinct and the fence posts discontinue. Continue SW through marshy hillocks and between rocky outcrops

Sergeant Man

towards the picturesque ponds of summit number 18 – Sergeant Man, a mountain in miniature.

From here, head NW on a large, straight track over very level ground towards the broad summit of High Raise (19). The ground can be a little boggy initially. From the High White Stones at High Raise, it's directly due south on a good fast path, descending slightly towards the head of Bright Beck. Where the path turns left (SE) for Pavey Ark, head across rocky ground for the summit cairn at Thunacar Knott (20).

From here, pick your way SSE over the broken rocks towards summit 21 – Harrison Stickle. The approach is marked with a cairn, where walkers can leave a backpack. There's an easy gully on the right-hand side, leading to a final few metres which can barely be described as a scramble (more of a clamber) and the summit itself. Backpackers can return to the cairn before heading west to Pike o' Stickle, but runners may descend steeply on a more direct path to meet some stepping-stones near the top of Dungeon Ghyll. From here, head directly west on the renovated path to Pike o' Stickle's summit (22). Another easy scramble, this time up a diagonal to a shoulder, and easier still without backpacks.

At the foot of the Pike, contour around on a bony, stony path which takes you North, climbing a little before dropping NW towards the wide expanse of Martcrag Moor.

At this point, runners may wish to head off the main path, following a smaller path west that cuts off the extra mileage around Langdale Combe. Skirting to the north of Mart Crag itself, descend in a direct line on sometimes boggy ground to the top of the steep section of Stake Pass. Cross the beck (a good water source) and the Cumbria Way at around NR 260 081 and head up between Black Crags and Mansey Pike, following a path marked with occasional cairns WSW to reach a shelf. This leads to the col NE of Rossett Pike. From the col (to the right of Black Crags) it's a short distance SW on a broad ridge to the increasingly rocky summit of Rossett Pike.

For backpackers not keen on losing the height with a load, the 'long way round' is perfectly acceptable and offers consolation in some great views from Mansey Pike. The path over Martcrag Moor is indistinct until the head of Stake Pass, after which it becomes clearer. Head over Mansey on a clear path SW for the summit (23) of Rossett Pike, a magical jumble of granite spikes.

The outflow of Angle Tarn provides a usable water source, and sheltered camping can be had nearby.

From the tarn, runners will ascend a beautiful but often vague path through diagonal slabs and screes on the North face of Bowfell. First, cross the path that comes up from Rossett Gill and head straight towards the face over broken ground towards a spring and a terrace (marked 'Hanging Knotts' on the 1:25K). Walk along the terrace to find a path with occasional small cairns. It's tempting to veer off the path to the right in the mistaken belief that you will miss the summit, but stick to it to achieve a small grassy col, turning left to clamber over the final metres of blocks to the summit (24) of Bowfell.

In bad weather or with heavy bags, those not aiming for a 24-hour round could choose the more conventional walker's route on the shoulder to the NW of Angle Tarn, which then heads south to Ore Gap, where you can leave bags could be left and pick them up on your return. However, in fine weather the direct runner's route described above is by far the more rewarding.

From the top of Bowfell, some of the highest and most dramatic ground in the Lake District stretches out west in front of you. Descend NW to Ore Gap and then on a good but stony path, climb to summit 25 – Esk Pike. The descent from this top is a beautiful trail giving rough but rewarding passage and grandstand views of what lies ahead. Now heading NNW, descend to the flatter, grassy plains of Esk Hause. Take the path west for a short while until it bends south, and then peel off NW again, climbing up through screes to the flat boulder summit (26) of Great End. Wainwright reckons the nearer top is the true one. See if you can find 'the coffin' – compact and bijou, sleeps one, no advance booking required!

The Mountain Rescue box at Mickledore, with Broad Stand behind

From the summit of Great End, take a simple and direct line south to rejoin the main path at the col. Backpackers can drop their bags for the out-and-back to the very rocky plateau summit of Ill Crag (27), before heading NW again and doing the same again for the more demanding (but still straightforward) scramble up to Broad Crag's summit (28). This is definitely easier without a load, as the boulders are big and sometimes loose.

From Broad Crag descend over more boulders, following a clear, cairned path on a narrowing ridge SW towards England's highest mountain and Bob Graham's summit number 29 – Scafell Pike. The ridge ascent is made up of eroded rocks and scree, but is pathed and straightforward.

From the summit of Scafell Pike, follow the main path down NW for a few metres, before peeling off SW on an intermittent but cairned path descending towards the col between the two Scafells, marked Mickeldore. Pass the Mountain Rescue stretcherbox, and aim directly ahead for the huge wall of Broad Stand.

Runners attempting the 24-hour round often go straight up here, sometimes with the use of a pre-arranged top rope and a friend to assist. With or without a top rope, rock climbing skills are essential for this option – holds are slim and the area exposed, as Coleridge discovered in 1802. It is classed as a Difficult rock climb and is an accident black spot. If you are prepared, the way ahead is not busy and conditions are suitable to ascend, go through a chimney in the rock to reach a platform, then ascend on smooth slabs heading to the right.

Other options are Lord's Rake and Wainwright's West Wall Traverse, but be aware that the latter is also an accident black spot (with Bob Graham contenders involved in a Mountain Rescue callout in the past).

The route shown on the map in this book – by way of Foxes Tarn – is the best option for most people. Standing in front of Broad Stand, take the path descending SE (which leads to Cam Spout) for a few metres. Take care not to walk past the outflow of Foxes Tarn; instead, scramble up the side of this small stream using the intermittent paths either side of it. Locate the tarn itself in a small bowl (sometimes soiled, so worth treating if you are using for drinking water!) and continue up NNW

on very loose and eroded scree interspersed with some old repaired sections of path. Top out on level grass, and turn SW for summit 30 – Scafell.

The beginning of the descent is obvious, but Green How can be confusing even in fair weather, so care is required for the next section. Return for a few metres back the way you came, then turn WNW for a cairned scree path. It's steep, loose and braided. It's best to take the main right-hand braid, which handrails the edge of the plateau (approximately 50m from the lip), as the left-hand path becomes vague and fizzles out at the head of Green How. Slowly, the path becomes more visible as the angle of descent eases and the going underfoot becomes grassy.

Runners have often favoured a final descent by the red scree shoot in front of Rakehead Crag (approximately NY 195 068 – on the map it's labelled, 'runner's option (eroded)' to access the lower part of the main path running alongside Lingmell Gill, but this is now extremely eroded and not at all recommended, and especially not for walkers and backpackers. If you are using this, it's still very steep after the scree runs out. Follow the line of the drystone wall, to cross Lingmell Gill and descend by the main path to the car park.

Most will be content to continue around Rakehead Crag and find the steep pathed descent, which runs alongside a stream at approximately NY 190 066. This can take some doing, as the route quickly becomes more of a trod after Rakehead Crag. Find the head of the stream, and go down on its left side, crossing three working stiles, which carry you across the fences and stone walls, through a scrubby, wooded area and into **Wasdale**. If you fail to find the stream, continue on around to the main Hardrigg Gill path, which comes off Scafell to the SW to meet Burnmoor Tarn. It's much longer but also a clearer route off, especially in poor visibility.

Runners should head into the Brackenclose car park, the usual changeover point. Take extra care not to disturb the other users of the car park and campsite, and please make sure all your support has paid the parking fee.

For walkers and backpackers, Wasdale Head, with its campsite, outdoor shop and excellent inn, offers a multitude of earthly delights!

Descending into Wasdale

Red Pike from Black Comb

LEG 4

Wasdale to Honister Pass

Distance	10.4 miles (16.7km)
Ascent	6167ft (1880m)

This leg involves a tough climb out of Wasdale; it's a challenging leg with some very loose ground underfoot, though it's not as long as leg 3. The high ridge circuit between Wasdale and Ennerdale is magnificent in every direction. After Great Gable, Haystacks and Borrowdale consistently draw the eye west.

The first climb out of Wasdale is very steep, especially with a bag. For walkers who cannot persuade their legs up the east flank of Yewbarrow, head SW on the road out of Wasdale until the car park at Bowderdale, and the more usual way up this beautiful hill. It's longer, but the views (if not the roadwalking) do justify the extra mileage. There is a footpath on the right before the car park itself, which enables you to cut a corner (and get off the road).

For those on the clock, from the bridge over Lingmell Beck (NY 181 075), head to the main Wasdale road and turn left. Go along the road for a short distance until you reach a gate marked 'Private'. As the signage will tell you, this next short section isn't on core access land, so your upmost care and discretion is advised. Go over this and ascend left to where the wall is replaced by a fence. Cross a stile and go straight up keeping the stream on your right. About halfway up, cross the stream and walk past a square block of rock, reach a flattish area, and where the trod splits take the left fork. Ascend NW (right) contouring until the route levels out, then turn left for the final few metres to summit number 31 – Yewbarrow.

From here, head NE along the broad ridge of the hill. To avoid the scramble at Stirrup Crag at the north end of Yewbarrow, keep an eye out for a small cairn on the saddle between the north and south top. Take a left here and head west off the ridge, under the crags, on a beautiful high trail, which hugs the mountain side. This is dirt at first, with the occasional rocky intersection. It splits halfway along: Take the right fork to stay high until you reach the pools of Dore Head.

Follow the path NW up to the next summit (32) – Red Pike – which is a long but simple climb over rocky terraces and grass. If the weather is benign there is good camping nearby, with Low and Scoat Tarns providing water in the wonderfully remote feeling country.

From Red Pike, head north on a clear path along the ridge for the next two tops. Runners may want to aim directly for the ridge, onto the outlier summit (33) of Steeple, before bypassing Scoat Fell (on the 1:25K OS map, named Little Scoat Fell) to the west.

Backpackers may find it far simpler to stay on the path as it curls around Black Comb, meet the path for Steeple on the east side of (Little) Scoat Fell, drop bags and visit both tops. From this side, head through a gap in the stone wall, follow the wall to a cairn, then drop down onto the Steeple ridge itself. Return by the ridge, this time following the wall over the summit of Scoat Fell.

After Steeple, head ENE, taking extra care with footfall on the eroded path from Black Crag to Wind Gap, down to the col of Wind Gap, before tackling the steep and stony ascent of summit number 34 – Pillar. This is a huge dome offering superb views in all direction, replete with several shelters, a cairn and a trig point.

By this point, the huge bulk of Great Gable to the southeast might well be dominating your thoughts, but there's still a fair bit of ground to cover beforehand. Descend on a lovely high ridge with views overlooking Ennerdale, to an alpine style high pasture, before meeting another precipitous hanging path that leads down to the **Black Sail Pass**. Collect water if needed, by dropping a few metres on the east side.

The most direct way to ascend Kirk Fell is to follow the fence posts straight to the top, although another path climbs through loose scree and shales on the NE side of the hill. Once out of these easy gullies, regain the fence posts and follow them to the summit (35) of Kirk Fell.

From the top, head NE, aiming off to the right of Kirkfell tarn at approximately NY 197 105 to regain the path, over spot height 787m and then due east again down steeply on screes to the col of Beck Head.

Here, Great Gable gives a different aspect – no longer a dome, rather more elongated. It's still big! Ascend on a clear path on the NW ridge, which occasionally makes small switchbacks on stony and increasingly loose ground, but is straightforward enough. Soon, you'll meet the Westmorland Memorial Cairn on summit 36 – Great Gable.

From the memorial, follow the cairns NE before descending very steeply, taking care on a very eroded and loose path. When you reach the col, it's a short but simple ascent via eroded red stone to the summit (37) of Green Gable.

From the top of Green Gable, descend gradually, NE, taking care to use a left fork (in a more northerly line). Follow the fence posts. Cairns will soon appear, and the ground becomes much easier and grassier underfoot. Head straight north, past the pools of Gillercomb (good camping and water) and over summit number 38 – Brandreth.

From Brandreth, follow the fence line NE towards the summit (39) of Grey Knotts, a beguiling area to wander through if you have the time. The National Park authority has concerns about runners choosing a grassy descent into Honister here, since it appears to be causing erosion. For the future of the Round, it may be best to opt for the path, keeping the fence on your left-hand side. This is steep and also eroded in places.

Pull up at the café (if open) for refreshments and runner's changeover. Note that the café will not fill water bottles, but these can be filled from the toilets. Please be mindful of the general public.

Great Gable from Kirk Fell (leg 4)

Honister Pass

LEG 5

Honister Pass to Keswick

Distance	10.5 miles (16.8km)
Ascent	2611ft (800m)

Going clockwise, the final leg is over easier, more rolling terrain again, first overlooking and then descending into the wonderfully picturesque Newlands valley. Runners may be tempted to maintain or increase their pace but be aware that the final section will see you cross paths with more of the public on your way into Keswick. Keep eating, and pace yourself!

Cross the road and head north on an easy path. The ascent on a broad ridge is gradual, not technical but can seem long! There's a fence to handrail but the path is mostly obvious to summit number 40 – Dale Head. At the cairn, admire the views over **Derwent Water**.

From here, it's all fairly easy going. Head west (left) along Hindscarth Edge for breezy views of Fleetwith Pike, before tackling Hindscarth. Runners will no doubt opt for the first path north to the top, whereas backpackers might choose to wait for the T-junction, and drop their sack before jogging to the summit (41) of **Hindscarth**. There are two tops here – the first is the highest.

Head back to collect your bags if necessary or contour around Little Dale, before heading ENE for the last climb of the Round. Summit number 42 – **Robinson** – offers great views of the **Derwent Fells**.

From the broad top, head NE as the ridge narrows to a lovely and engaging descent with two or three interesting scrambles. This is not technical, but backpackers may want to put poles away. Continue to the col below a steep section (NY 212 177) where it's possible to drop off the ridge early to the tarn below, or carry on over Blea Crags for the grassy High Snab Bank. At the Y in the path,

descend steeply east with a line of trees on your left.

Join a charming track and, still heading NE, pass High Snab itself. Follow the lanes to Newlands Church. At the T-junction, turn right and pass the car park.

If time is tight, you may choose to use the roads for this final section into Keswick. There is a more scenic route with less tarmac that takes us via Yewthwaite mines (labelled 'walker's option' on the map). Around 50m beyond the car park, look for a railing on your right. Take this path, go over a stile and up a few steps to a track. Go right (back on yourself) for around 150m, before taking a left on a grassy track heading NE again. Follow this track around to Skelgill, and then the car park at the foot of **Catbells**.

Taking care not to take the path up Catbells, follow the road left for a short time, go over a cattle grid, and take the signed turning for Hawesend

The Newlands Valley

Launch Pier. Shortly afterwards, go through a gate signed for Portinscale and take a long track. This takes you past Lingholm estate, where more signage beckons you on to Keswick.

Take a left fork following the Cumbria Way, through the woods to join the road into **Portinscale** itself. At the junction, take a right, signposted footpath over the suspension bridge (Stormwater Bridge) and then follow the riverside path, through gates and across a pasture with fences on either side of the path.

When you enter **Keswick**, turn left to cross the stone bridge and head straight through town to finish the Bob Graham Round, at the **Moot Hall**.

Congratulations!

Practicalities

Getting there and around

By road, Keswick is accessed on the A66 from Penrith, which in turn sits on the M6 between Lancaster and Carlisle. This is the main trunk road on the west side of the country. From London and the south, take the M40 to Birmingham before joining the M42 and then the M6. If you intend to run these rounds, you will get to know the M40 almost as well through reconnoitring trips! From the southwest, take the M5 to Birmingham. From the north, take the M74 south in the first instance.

Public transport is a good option, too. There are regular and direct trains from London, Manchester, Edinburgh and Glasgow to Penrith, 17 miles from Keswick. The X5 bus connects Penrith rail station to Keswick Bus Station and takes around 40 minutes.

From the bus station opposite Booths, go NE up Headlands a short distance to join Heads road on your right. Continue left onto Main Street to turn right at the roundabout. Now walk straight ahead (also called Main Street) for a few hundred metres. Ignoring the road turning left (now Bank Street) continue in a straight line through the pedestrianised area to arrive at the Moot Hall. This takes around 10 minutes.

Water

The following is a list of places where stream or tarn water may be found to refill your bottle. These and other points are also noted in the full route notes. Be aware that this is wild water and may well need treating, especially in the Lakes, where visitor pressure and a lack of good outdoors education has led to contamination, even high on the hillside.

Leg 1
- Whit Beck, on the climb of Skiddaw Little Man.
- Wiley Gill Confluence, after Great Calva.

Leg 2
- Tributary feeding Mosedale Beck, east of Calfhow Pike.
- Grisedale Tarn and tributaries running off both east and west (treatment highly recommended).

Leg 3

- Mere Beck, after Calf Crag.
- Langdale Comb, after Pike o' Stickle.
- Angle Tarn and tributaries (treatment highly recommended).

Leg 4

- Tarn at Dore Head, after Yewbarrow.
- Stream at Black Sail Pass, after Pillar.
- Water at Beck Head, after Kirk Fell.
- Tarns at Grey Knotts.

Leg 5

- River at Scope Beck, after Robinson.

Suggested backpacker's itinerary

The beauty of wild camping is that it can happen anywhere (within reason and the law), and I am wary of supplying times, because everyone's pace is different. Overly specific information can lead some to make dangerous assumptions in the mountains. However, here is a guide that may be useful.

Day 1

- A longish first day, from Keswick to the Old Coach Road, near or under Clough Head (near the start of Stage 2).

Day 2

- A shorter second day, from the Dodds and Helvellyn down to Grisedale Tarn.

Day 3

- One big ascent and some complex navigation, from Grisedale Tarn to the Langdales.

Day 4

- A shorter day but over the highest, most exposed ground on the round, from the Langdales to Wasdale.

Day 5

- A big climb out from Wasdale and along to Grey Knotts, above Honister Pass. A fairly tough section.

Day 6

- A shorter, less arduous section to finish, from Grey Knotts back to Keswick.

Alternative ways to complete the Bob Graham Round

Because the Lakes have much simpler access than either of the other two Rounds, suggestions for breaking up the journey into further legs seem almost redundant, but here are a few, very subjective suggestions. Arguably, these turn the Bob Graham Round into something of a 10-day 'luxury' walking holiday with a few scrambles and plenty of catered sleeping and eating options. This is a long way from the grit and grind of a sub 24-hour round, but there are some advantages to this way of tackling the same ground. It may involve more descent and re-ascent and take much longer, but you'll get to see more of the area, get hands-on with some of the iconic ridgelines and support the local economy into the bargain.

Leg 1: The hills north of Keswick

All of stage 1 can comfortably be completed using Keswick or Threlkeld as a base should you wish, and I've enjoyed doing this in the past with only a day sack for the scrambles. The bus service X5 Penrith to Keswick can be useful to shuttle you along the A66, should you wish to tackle Sharp Edge in ascent (not on the Bob Graham), as well as Hall's Fell in descent.

Great Calva is an outlier, but if you fancy staying somewhere different, Skiddaw House, an independent bunkhouse, is relatively nearby (details below).

Leg 2: The eastern ridge – the Dodds, Helvellyn and Fairfield

This section could be broken down further without carrying extra kit, by dropping down to Glenridding via Swirral Edge (a sub grade 1 scramble) off Helvellyn, where there is a campsite and other places to stay. This would allow a resupply should you need it, but also a re-ascent of the ridge by way of Striding Edge, a grade 1 scramble. From here, it would be possible to extend the round south a little and using part of the famous Fairfield 'horseshoe' route, drop down into Grasmere for more food and accommodation options, including another youth hostel (details below). This leaves Seat Sandal out though, so instead you could choose to come off the south side of Seat Sandal via Tongue Gill and drop down to the pub before the last of the road walk into town. Getting back up to the Dunmail Raise for the beginning of leg 3 might require the use of the bus 555 north on the A591.

Leg 3: The high ground

The area between Dunmail Raise and Wasdale is probably best divided into two for day-trippers, and easily split at Langdale, where there is a great pub (the Old Dungeon Gyll) and a great campsite (details below). The aforementioned bar was the venue for the first Bob Graham reunion dinner in 1971, at which the formation of the 24-hour club was decided.

Come off the plateau after either Harrison Stickle or Pike o' Stickle. If you do the latter, then you can re-join the Round the following day by heading NW on the Cumbria Way and climbing back up to Rossett Pike by way of Rossett Gill, at the head of the valley. Be aware that by adding in the descent and re-ascent from Langdale, this section still equates to two longish and challenging days.

Leg 4: Wasdale circuits

Another good campsite (details below) and historic drinking den make the valley of Wasdale a good base for an exploration of the Western Fells. The circuit of Mosedale, from Yewbarrow to Black

Haystacks and Fleetwith Pike, from Brandreth

Sail Pass is a full day for most hillwalkers, and Kirkfell, Great Gable and Green Gable can also be accessed easily. The Black Sail Hut at the head of Ennerdale can also be used as a good base for these hills, although it does involve a descent and reascent of about 280m back up to Black Sail Pass.

Leg 5: Honister Pass and Derwent Fells

The Pass is a pretty bleak place to stay, but the YHA there could be useful to access Brandreth and Grey Knotts, as well as provide a jumping off point for the Derwent Fells to the north – Dale Head, Hindscarth and Robinson – also on the Round. For those arriving in the day without support, the café can be pretty handy too.

Off the Round, there's plenty to be said for exploring nearby Buttermere and Ennerdale, although the campsite down in Buttermere would arguably be a more pleasant place to do that from.

The Derwent Fells can also be accessed simply from the car parks at Little Town and Newlands Hause on the minor road between Keswick and Buttermere.

Places to stay and resupply

Here are a few campsite and youth hostel locations, which may be useful if you are planning to 'section' the round or need to accommodate support teams, as well as shop information. There is more information about nearby towns and villages in the preceding section.

Leg 1
- Numerous B&Bs, hotels and eateries at both Keswick and Threlkeld (en route).
- Skiddaw House is usefully situated for Skiddaw and Great Calva, and would make for a fun way to start the round if not on the clock (off route). Web: www.skiddawhouse.co.uk; tel: 07747 174293; email: info@skiddawhouse.co.uk.

Leg 2
- Glenridding, Gillside campsite (off route). Web: www.gillsidecaravanandcampingsite. co.uk; tel: 017684 82346; email: gillside@ btconnect.com.

- Grasmere YHA (off route). Web: www.yha.org. uk/hostel/grasmere-butharlyp-howe; tel: 015394 35245; email: grasmere@yha.org.uk.
Both Glenridding and Grasmere have small food stores.

Leg 3
- Great Langdale National Trust Campsite (off route). Web: www.nationaltrust.org. uk/features/great-langdale-campsite; tel: 015394 37668; email: see above to make a booking.
- Wasdale National Trust Campsite (en route). Web: www.nationaltrust.org.uk/features/ wasdale-campsite; tel: 01946 726220; email: see above to make a booking.
Both have small food supply shops connected to the campsite, and pubs nearby serving food.

Leg 4
- Honister Pass YHA (en route). Web: www.yha. org.uk/hostel/honister-hause; tel: +44 345 371 9522; email: honister@yha.org.uk.
- Syke Farm Campsite, Buttermere (off route). Web: www.sykefarmcampsite.com; tel: 017687 70222; email: info@sykefarmcampsite. com.
- Black Sail YHA (off route). Web: www.yha.org. uk/hostel/black-sail; tel: +44 345 371 9680; email: blacksail@yha.org.uk.

Support for runners

The following is a list of the most commonly used spots for support vehicles supplying food, drink and pacer changes. There are specific challenges regarding access on the Round.

Start and finish
- The Moot Hall is in the centre of a busy high street in a bustling town. Please be mindful of market traders, pedestrians and residents when leaving and arriving in town. Participants on the Round are ambassadors for the sport of hill running, and the Bob Graham is not a race. It's also worth noting that public drinking is prohibited by bylaw, so celebrations should wait until away from the Moot Hall.

Wasdale at Sunset

Leg 2 – Threlkeld

- The changeover for runners is usually either in front of the industrial unit above the village, or on the verge of the A66. There are no toilets. This is a residential area, so please keep noise to a minimum and don't crowd the area with vehicles.

Leg 3 – Dunmail Raise

- The verge at Dunmail Raise, the highest point on the main north-south road in the lakes, the A591. No toilets.

Leg 4 – Wasdale

- The National Trust car park at Brackenclose, Wasdale is most often used as a support point. All visitors must pay and display. Bob Graham contenders and club members are not exempt.

Only National Trust members with proof of their membership are permitted to park here for free. Please also bear in mind that there is a campsite next door, so keep noise to an absolute minimum, especially if you are on an overnight changeover. No shelters or awnings are permitted in the car park, and if your support teams are using the camp ground overnight, then you will need to pay as a normal customer and abide by the same regulations as other visitors.

This changeover has been a point of friction for the Round in the past, so your and your team's understanding is essential in order that the Bob Graham Round continues to flourish for other runners in the future. Portaloos are usually present in the summer months.

the Moot Hall, in the centre of Keswick, and it can be run either clockwise or anticlockwise.

The club asks that all attempts are registered with the membership secretary ahead of time, and that after a successful attempt a detailed report is sent to the same. It should include your full name, the date of the attempt, a full schedule (time at each summit, the start and end of each rest period), the names of all pacers and supporters, as well as a written account. Email communication is to be sent to membership@bobgraham club.org.uk, and archive@bobgrahamclub.org.uk.

Solo attempts are not accepted, and will not be ratified by the club. Runners are required to be accompanied by pacers who witness their arrival on each summit, and provide both moral support and a safety net should anyone's health or the mountain conditions deteriorate. Adhering to these rules means that some risk is mitigated while leaving the challenge intact. It also demonstrates the need for structure and planning in an attempt, as well as encouraging mutual support in the fell running community. The club advises that two pacers and witnesses per stage or leg are usually sufficient, and that if the team splits up over the course of the Round, then ratification will not be granted.

There are three further points of guidance that are worth mentioning here:

- The club expressly forbids any pre-marking of the route.

- It also forbids the pre-fixing of climbing gear on the technical crux, Broad Stand. There are more details about both elsewhere in this book.

- The club also make a distinction between a 'mid-winter' round and a 'winter' round. A winter round for the Bob Graham Club is the same as it is for the Ramsay Round – a successful run between 1 December and the end of February – regardless of conditions, which of course can be included in the runner's report. A mid-winter round is defined as being from the weekend before 21 December until 10 January.

Leg 5 – Honister Pass
- The car park behind the Youth Hostel. Be respectful of other visitors. The use of toilets in the café has sometimes proved contentious.

Rules for runners

The Bob Graham Round is the round that birthed the others in this book, and the guidance for running it as a timed challenge is the simplest of the three.

The Bob Graham 24 Hour Club seeks to support contenders in their timed attempts and members are the custodians of the traditions, ethics and reputation of the Round. Their rules are clear: membership of the club will be granted to anyone who completes the full round of 42 summits within 24 hours. The route starts and finishes at

The history of the Round

The Bob Graham Round is nowadays looked after by a club, and that means the criteria for a successful timed round are the most formalised of all three. But it wasn't always this way. The history of the Round is about both the making and the breaking of boundaries, and the early pioneers were just as motivated to go further and faster as many contenders are today. The Bob Graham may have become the benchmark challenge, but for some it is also part of a continuum, the gateway to more. And the club's traditions contain the seeds of further challenges (only two of which are covered here)...with the push for the greatest number of Lakeland hills within 24 hours being the most obvious 'other'. We look briefly at some of these other challenges in Appendix D.

Before Bob Graham himself, there were other giants, and other shoulders to stand on. A shorter round of the Wasdale fells was first recorded in around 1864, by a Cambridgeshire vicar, the Rev. JM Elliot. A few years later, Darlington-based Thomas Watson did something more like what we think of as the Bob Graham Round, starting and finishing in Keswick and aiming to visit all the 3000ft peaks. With a Borrowdale guide, he covered 48 miles in under 20 hours. In 1902, the record was furthered by SB Johnson of Carlisle, who achieved 70 miles and 18,000ft of ascent in a time of 22hr 30min.

So, by around the turn of the 20th century, there was already a precedent for the 'most hills in a day'. But it was a man called Dr Wakefield who Roger Smith, author of *42 Peaks – the Story of the Bob Graham Round*, reckons 'can fairly be called the first modern contender'. Wakefield was already a noted mountaineer in 1903, when he set a record of 21 peaks over 2000ft in a little over 22 hours. In the following years, he finessed the

Bob Graham and pacers at Dunmail in 1932. © Abraham Photographic

On the Langdales, leg 3

record several times, running a course remarkably similar to the modern Round, and doing so in lightweight kit: a rugby shirt, shorts and gym shoes. It's interesting that Fairfield is included even at this early stage, as it's not quite 3000ft and stands apart from the rest of the Eastern fells, some of which Wakefield omits as well.

Wakefield later went on to become part of the 1922 Everest expedition, but two years before that, Eustace Thomas ran the route in 21hr 25min, proving he'd been paying attention to Wakefield's own coaching! A year later, in 1921, Thomas added in the ridge north of Helvellyn ('the Dodds') that often forms the night section for those running anticlockwise today, upping the number of hills climbed from 21 to 28. Thomas used nailed boots for his attempt, although he later gave them up and designed the shoes that Roger Bannister used for the first sub 4-minute mile.

A decade passed, and there were other attempts on the record that met without success. In 1931, former gardener and Keswick guest house owner Bob Graham tried for the Eustace Thomas record, but bad weather and navigation issues thwarted his attempt. According to one of his pacers – Phil Davidson – Bob Graham was

41 at the time. A year later and he apparently felt the need to add another hill to the itinerary to match his years; it was Great Calva, at the back of Skiddaw. No wonder it feels a little arbitrary!

A year older and perhaps a little wiser, Bob Graham and his first pacer Martin Ryland set out at 1am on Sunday 13 June 1932, having called off an attempt the previous weekend due to bad weather. They travelled clockwise, after taking advice from the well-known mountaineer and photographer George Abraham. He was waiting at Dunmail Raise alongside Phil Davidson, who joined them before Abraham took his somewhat auspicious photograph of the team standing together.

They added in the Langdale Pikes and High Raise for the first time, with another pacer, Robin Deans, joining them for leg 4 from Wasdale. The group made it back to the Moot Hall in 23hr 39min, setting a new benchmark of 42 peaks in less than 24 hours, and a record that lasted for 28 years.

For training prior to the event, Bob and his companions famously did little more than take extended fell walks, some of which went through the night. For the attempt itself, he wore tennis shoes, shorts and a pyjama top and ate bread and butter, a boiled egg, fruit and sweets. It's become the stuff of legend, but as Roger Smith notes, at the time there was some doubt about the veracity of his claim for the record, and of the distance covered (which was vastly overestimated by the press).

Graham is supposed to have said: 'Anyone can do it, as long as they are fit enough.' But no one did, or could, for another generation. In the late 1950s, as the country came up for air after World War 2, long-distance walking became popular and more people took to the hills for recreation and relaxation. In particular, the Land's End to John o' Groats route became well known, but Harry Griffin, a columnist for the *Lancashire Evening Post*, wrote a piece about Graham's record reminding readers what a 'real' challenge looked like.

Journalists play minor supporting roles in all Big Three Rounds; in some ways, Griffin's role of provocateur is similar to Chris Brasher for the Paddy Buckley Round, and Tom Weir and Chris again for the Charlie Ramsay Round...but more of that later.

Griffin's treatise caught the attention of two local mountaineering brothers, Alan and Ken Heaton, both of whom were also members of running club Clayton-le-Moors Harriers in Lancashire. They weren't alone. Maurice Collett and Paul Stewart tried getting around faster than Graham in May 1960, but bad weather hampered their efforts, resulting in a still respectable time of 27hr 20min.

The record was still intact, but not for long. Around a month later, the Heaton brothers set off at 10am on an anticlockwise schedule of 23hr 30min. Roger Smith's account of their attempt in *42 Peaks* makes for a gripping read, featuring a split support team, broken spectacles, injury, dehydration and cramps, but the pair made it in a time of 22hr 18min, taking an hour off Graham's record. It could be done. The Rounds are not a race, but the race was now on!

Stan Bradshaw completed the round successfully in under 24 hours, a mere two weeks after pacing the Heaton brothers, but the following attempts were all focused on raising the number of peaks – just as it had been in the past. In 1961,

Ken Heaton managed 51 peaks, and a year later, his brother Alan pushed the envelope to 54.

For the first of these and for the first time, the logistics of support were organised by a local hill-walker, inspired by the brothers' achievements. Fred Rogerson became the de facto book-keeper for the record attempts from that point on and a decade later, suggested a club be formed to celebrate the achievements of the contenders, and support others in their attempts.

In January 1971, at a reunion dinner in the Old Dungeon Ghyll Hotel in Langdale, the idea of a club was decided, and later that year its aims were agreed. They are worth reprinting here in full:

- To specify and define the 42 summits traversed by Bob Graham during his round of the fells within 24 hours.
- To provide intending qualifying members with all details and relevant information.
- To encourage and advise intending members before, and possibly during attempts.
- To record all registered attempts.

At that point, there were still only four individuals who'd successfully got round in under 24 hours, but despite never running the Round himself, Fred became the first chairman of the club. For many years he met runners on their round attempt to lend his support and encouragement, often at Dunmail Raise. He died in 2010 but is remembered with huge affection.

The Round is still looked after and administered by the Bob Graham 24-hour Club, which is free to join providing you have fairly navigated over Graham's 42 hills in less than 24 hours. Chris Brasher, who features in the story of every one of the Big Three, famously remarked that the Bob Graham Club was the most exclusive club in the world, because membership could not be bought.

A runner's story: Rob Bushby

Rob ran his Bob Graham in August 1994 in a time of 23hr 08min, becoming club member number 896. He ran anticlockwise – the opposite direction to the route described in this book – and this is his joyful and frank account.

'Rather you than me!' was the common response to the mention of a Bob Graham Round attempt. This was quickly followed by a questioning approach to my mental state of health. Struggling up Kirk Fell, with 34 Lakeland peaks still to surmount, I was inclined to agree with the sceptics. Having just jettisoned the pasta choice I'd been force-fed at Honister Pass I enquired of Brian, my veteran pacer: 'Should I be feeling a bit tired by now?' 'I suppose so,' he replied, 'but chucking your guts up just then wasn't a good sign. Have another jelly baby.'

It appeared to me that Bob Graham attempts fell into two camps: those who undergo months of focused training, back-up planned with military precision, and those who wake up one morning, think 'I fancy having a go at that Bob Graham thing', then go out and do it. Membership of the exclusive club requires the traverse of 42 Lake District peaks, covering about 61 miles, within 24 hours. As such, the former strategy has much to commend it. Deciding on an attempt only one week previously, however, meant that the ad hoc last-minute approach was the one I adopted.

I'd been intrigued by the notion (if not the reality) of the Bob Graham Round for a couple of years. A continuous circuit of the major mountain ranges of the Lake District had a strong aesthetic appeal, with the varied terrain and changing character being viewed in a kind of 24-hour omnibus

Mac n' cheese at Honister Pass © Rob Bushby collection

edition. To see the distant outline of Blencathra and Skiddaw from Scafell, then proceed towards them for 12 hours or so, gives a perspective that combines panorama and intimacy, a fuller experience and closer relationship with the mountains. Then there was the personal aspect. Was it beyond my running abilities? To what extent was it to be a mental, rather than a physical challenge? Was I scared to make a commitment just because of the fear of failing? I knew that the answers would never become clear unless I gave it a go.

A weekend identified itself – work-free, full moon and a few people around to help. There were lots of opt-out clauses: minimal training, long-distance running inexperience and being generally knackered, but none of them were sufficiently convincing. All of the night-before preparation fell neatly into place, with a skeletal support team forming. Scepticism was balanced with advice and words of support:

- 'Drink and eat lots.'
- 'Take power bars and Lucozade.'
- 'Don't walk the uphill.'
- 'Use the fence posts on Great Calva's east side to drag yourself up – you'll need to by then!'
- 'Don't bonk for Britain tonight!'

The words of Fred Rogerson stuck with me: 'Take them one at a time and they'll fall, one by one. They'll fall.'

As I arrived with Rachael at Keswick Moot Hall, the whole experience seemed to be taking on an abstract sense, an isolated chapter removed from the everyday scheme of things. Local fell runner Mike Fanning appeared round the corner accompanied by a friend's dog, suffering from the after effects of a Friday-night curry. With a good luck peck (from my wife Rachael, not Mike), we were on our way, departing at the slightly incongruous time of 8.35am.

We set a steady pace along the roads towards Newlands valley. The grey morning carried a humid edge, which had me breaking a sweat already. I tapped Mike for advice to take my mind off what lay ahead. We maintained a steady jog up the inclines beyond Little Town, the first climb up to High Snab Bank pulling tautly on my calves. How will the rest of it be? I dismissed doubts, wouldn't let them linger. Several mist-laden false summits led to the top of Robinson. A skip of elation – first one down! And the time matched that of Paul Yardley, a BG graduate whose timesheet we'd brought for guidance. It was beginning to sink in that I was really doing it, here and now.

Hindscarth and Dale Head were quickly ticked off in refreshing light rain, which afforded occasional glimpses of Great Gable and its neighbours. We slipped down to Honister Pass with confidence raised, to be met by Rachael and a new pacing team. First stage over, and relatively painless too! I'd found a rhythm and shaken off

A recce of leg 5, Bob Graham Round

the earlier sluggishness – I never was a morning person – and was looking forward to cracking on.

Brian and Rich, colleagues from Outward Bound, readied themselves as Rachael smothered my feet with talc, changed my socks and fed me macaroni cheese. Mike bade farewell, with a promise to return that evening to see me over Helvellyn and the Dodds. Hurried from repose by the enthusiasm of my new team, a purposeful pace up Grey Knotts was a little too quick for comfort. As Great Gable approached I entered a phase of physical and mental torment. Three elements – legs, stomach and head – became distinctly unsynchronised. My legs felt strong, but my stomach churned like a spin drier and my mind was unfocused, lost and confused in abstract thoughts. I contemplated the round in terms of a pregnancy: this was the labour stage, discomfort, that would gradually degenerate into ongoing pain, until, with accelerated panting and effort, the whole thing would finally be over. I'd lost that sense of rhythm essential for covering distance, and became frustrated at the rugged terrain and my inability to run with anything other than stuttering steps.

An explosive chunder provided a timely cure, discarding the pasta choice and unifying my disparate faculties. Brian's pessimistic assessment

"My legs felt strong, but my stomach churned like a spin drier and my mind was unfocused, lost and confused in abstract thoughts."

of the situation did nothing for my confidence so I sucked on a jelly baby and kept quiet. The day's biggest challenge was trying to replace some lost energy by digesting a Snickers bar – it took half an hour and the whole of the ascent of Pillar. Then came a diversion to Steeple and a knee-jarring jog towards Yewbarrow. I was glad of its scrambling approach, and perked up at the simultaneous sight of another 'Bobber' and Wasdale Head. A steep and rapid descent, and we were at the end of leg 2, right on schedule.

The two litres of water and bread roll input at Wasdale must have been pumped with adrenalin; Scafell was afforded little fear and conquered in sure and steady style within the hour. This was a welcome psychological boost: sanity had returned and I was feeling strong. Brian was knackered by now though, and it was my turn to lend support. Better judgement steered us away from Broad Stand, and an elusive Lord's Rake lost us half an hour on our escape from the clouded summit. Time wasn't a big issue, though. We were virtually halfway around, I felt good, and was enjoying the day. We were told of a redheaded lass who was looking for us as we scampered up Mickledore, and caught up with Rachael on Scafell Pike at 978m, the highest point in England. It was a perfect time and place

Cofa Pike, on the route to Fairfield

to top up supplies, our jelly babies having run out on Scafell.

We detoured off the main drag to the summits of Broad Crag, Ill Crag and Great End, the weekend walkers largely oblivious to our efforts. The occasional hiker recognised the tell-tale pairing of one runner carrying all the gear and the other looking slightly more ragged, and enquired, 'Bob Graham? Good luck, mate, keep it up.' Bright evening sunlight peeped through from underneath heavy, threatening cumulus, giving lovely conditions for a gentle run up Bowfell. Brian's intuitive navigation enabled us to skirt above the southern flank of Angle Tarn to then take in the soggy, boggy approach towards the twin sentinels of the Langdale Pikes. The rocky climb to Pike o' Stickle and Harrison Stickle gave a secure, firm respite from the previous peaty shite, but reminded my legs that they were almost 12 hours into the event. I was encouraged by the onset of the final two sections – the welcome, familiar sight of the rolling Dodds were getting closer. I'd worry about Blencathra later. Brian and I weren't saying much; we didn't need to. His initial doubts had dissolved, and he transmitted a quiet confidence, continually nudging me along.

With the hills virtually to ourselves, we reached Steel Fell summit at dusk. A tricky descent to Dunmail Raise in rapidly fading light followed, guided by the lights of an expanded team below. I crossed the A591 at 9.30pm, skipping cockily to show off and say, 'Look, I'm still fresh and up to it.' Words of encouragement (and surprise!) at such positive progress became more purposeful as I lingered. Brian's prior pacing contributions had been for failed attempts and he was determined that this one would reward his efforts with success. I couldn't express my gratitude appropriately as he departed for home. He had been key in keeping me relaxed and confident and on course, both navigationally and timewise. The leg massage, foot rub and replenishment stop passed all too quickly.

Seat Sandal was a nightmare, a tortured 45 minutes. 'A bit of a grunt, this,' understated Mike as he resumed his pacing duties. The legs had forgotten about long steep uphills, the last significant ascent having been six hours earlier. And Fairfield and Dollywagon to follow, too! Their bark, in fact, was worse than their bite, the gradient seeming favourable after the front of Seat Sandal. A line straight down from Cofa Pike saved time and by 12.30am we were on top of Helvellyn.

A thick line of ticks now would keep morale up. The moon, full and brilliant, reminded us that it was there only as a favour, regularly dodging behind clouds.

Mike took his pathfinding responsibilities seriously, finding the most treacherous route across Sticks Pass and sinking up to his waist in bog. 'Avoid this bit here, Rob' was his generous advice. The undulating paths of the Dodds are a runner's dream: smooth, not too steep, and space, lots of open space. Mike looked after me like a dog on a lead, running ahead, then looking back to check that I was keeping up. A drenching on Great Dodd didn't dampen our spirits as we navigated intuitively towards Clough Head. The drop down to Threlkeld was arduous. My knees ached and my diaphragm felt bruised from all of the shaking about it had endured, making breathing difficult. ('You should have taken it out,' joked one wag). As we neared the lights of Newsham Farm, voices could be heard: 'Is that you Rob?' Who else would it be? Rachael had gathered a posse – Ann, fellow Outward Bound tutor, and a couple of her mates from Ambleside. 'Well, the video wouldn't work,' seemed a fair excuse for turning out at 3 in the morning.

Hall's Fell Ridge was longer than I'd remembered. After an hour of huffing and puffing, the summit of Blencathra came as a relief. By this stage energy conservation was a priority and conversation limited. I concentrated on nibbling at a power bar. Darkness was slowly lifting beyond Penrith as we encountered the long drag down Mungrisdale Common. Tussock and bog gave way to knee-deep heather, and the sting in the tail – Great Calva. Some poem or other ends with the line: 'Endure, endure, endure again, until endurance itself is beaten into joy.' What bollocks, I thought. From first examination of the route, I'd always seen this as a masochistic endeavour, a view confirmed by the strenuous yomp around to the recommended path and fence spikes to aid a rhythmic plod to the top. 41 down, only one to go!

I was determined to ignore any time pressure there might be, and ran purposefully until the obtuse tussocks reduced us to a stagger. Across Dead Beck and up the seemingly endless spur of Hare Crag, Ann and I matched each other stride for stride. The sun, fully risen now, cast a golden glow directly onto Skiddaw's flanks, and illuminated the lush purple heather. A warm sense of euphoria enveloped me as we made the final summit. Now, for the first time, I allowed myself the luxury of the knowledge that I was going to complete the Round. Rachael kept up her habit of popping up in odd places, and woke from an hour of slumber in the summit cairn shelter to check that we were OK. A few hundred metres of stiff-legged stagger yielded to a more fluid stride, and by the time we met Mike at Latrigg we were cruising. It took exactly an hour to reach the Moot Hall from the final peak.

Most journeys end where they begin: I touched the steps at 7.43am, completing in a respectable time of 23 hours and 8 minutes. This was cause for both celebration and relief – I'd dreaded the prospect of dragging myself to the finish in a desperate, ragged heap, so to still be upright and finishing in good style was a bonus.

"It had been the most enjoyable day I'd ever spent on the hill, shared with friends who'd given wonderful support."

Celebrations weren't really necessary. I hobbled to the paper shop and we adjourned to Mike's place for a brew. Mental and physical numbness were displaced by a tremendous sense of achievement. It had been the most enjoyable day I'd ever spent on the hill, shared with friends who'd given wonderful support. Before starting, I hadn't appreciated the full part their assistance would play in making the day such a success. It was very much a team effort rather than a solo endeavour, and I'm looking forward to continuing the tradition of assisting others in attempts to join the Bob Graham 24 Hour Club. It's a club that is exclusive, though not elite. To have followed, quite literally, in the footsteps of many respected runners and remarkable individuals and joined their club is a memorable and humbling experience. While the aches and pains were short-lived, the inner sense of accomplishment will always be there.

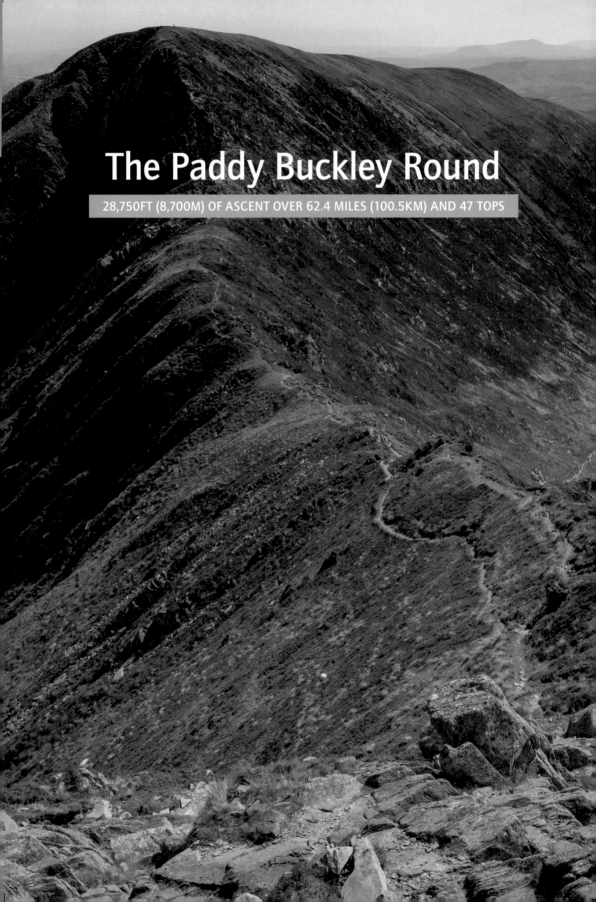

The Paddy Buckley Round

28,750FT (8,700M) OF ASCENT OVER 62.4 MILES (100.5KM) AND 47 TOPS

The steep descent to Bwlch Eryi Farchog (leg 5, Paddy Buckley Round)

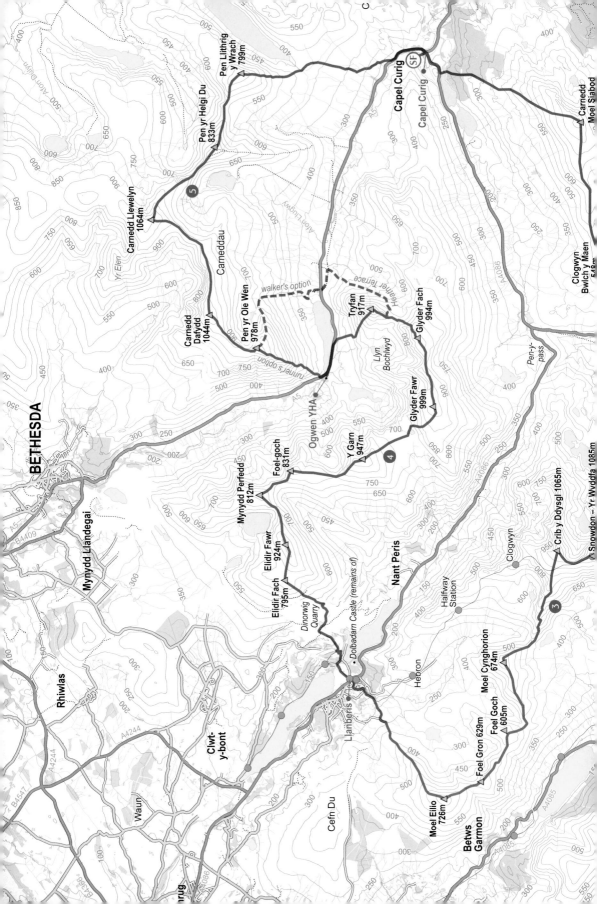

294

Dolwyddelan Castle

661

BLAENAU FFESTINIOG

LLAN FFESTINIOG

Congl-y-wal

Tanygrisiau

Vale of Ffestiniog

Tan y Bwich

Rhyd

Llanfrothen

Coed Llyn y Garnedd

Carnedd Y Cribau 591m

Cerrig Cochion 550m

Moel Meirch 607m

Mynydd Llynau yr Cwn 669m

Ysgafell Wen 650m

Llyn Edno

Allt Fawr 698m

Foel Ddu 458m

Moel yr hydd 648m

Moelwyn Bach 710m

Summit no.8 aka 'three tops' 672m

Moel Druman 676m

Llyn Conglog

Rhosydd Quarry

Moelwyn Mawr 770m

Craig Ysgafn 689m

walker's option

Cnicht 689m

Croesor

Bwlch Gwernog

Llyn Gwynant YHA & camping

Plas Gwynant

Afon Glaslyn

Beddgelert

Cribau Tregalan 931m

Yr Aran 747m

Craig Wen 608m

Pont Cae'r Gors

Nantmor

Afon Glaslyn

Bryn Banog 520m

Rhyd-Ddu

Beddgelert Forest

Mynydd Drws-y-Coed 695m

Y Gryn 452m

Moel Lefn 638m

Moel Hebog 782m

Y Garn 633m

Mynydd y Ddwy Elor 466m

Moel yr Ogof 655m

Trum y Ddysgl 709m

Afon Dwyfor

N

km

0   1   2

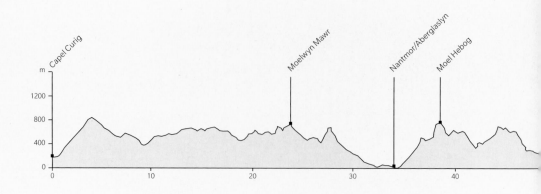

'Would you mind if I took your picture?'
'I couldn't give a monkey's – I'm too busy
trying to breathe!' A runner on Elidir Fawr

The Paddy Buckley Round was conceived as the Welsh answer to the Bob Graham Round and covers around 62 tough miles of rock, bog, heather and bracken. It passes through two slate mines and over the highest mountain in Wales – Yr Wyddfa, or Snowdon. It's the longest of the three rounds here – for runners it's reckoned to be longer than the Bob Graham by at least an hour on average. It includes more summits than the other two rounds – 47 in total – and arguably the most technical navigation.

Paddy and many other runners regard it as the most difficult of the three rounds. It has more ascent than the English round and less than the Scottish one. However, it's rarely as remote as the latter, and is far easier to access. For walkers and backpackers, the Paddy Buckley's roughness underfoot is somewhat mitigated by the fact that it can be easily split into sections, most or all with a B&B at the end of each day. It is possible to walk a multiday route with only a day sack if you wished, although it's useful to be able to bivi en route in a couple of places.

The Paddy Buckley Round sits entirely within the Snowdonia National Park in North Wales, which is a more compact area than the Lake District. The area is similarly shaped by farming but perhaps less so by tourism. Overall and by comparison to the Lakes, the region sees around one-fifth as many visitors a year, and they tend to congregate in the north of the park. The mountains south of the Ogwen Valley and around Snowdon itself (the busiest mountain in the UK, with its own railway and café, no less) are the

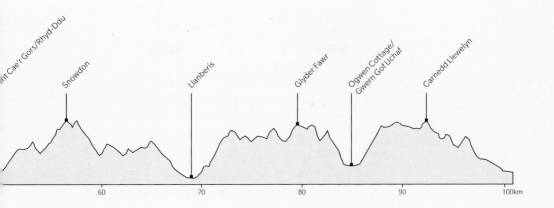

hotspots, although the Carneddau (on the north side of this valley) are becoming increasingly well-trod. The south and west of the Round are much quieter than the northern and central parts.

Once again, fire and ice have shaped the place, but there's a more widely spread mix of sedimentary, metamorphic and igneous rock across the region, and the terrain is generally more complex and undulating than on the Bob Graham as a result. Wildlife is in a marginally better state too, and includes otters, polecats and feral goats. The woods and hedgerows around Nantmor in the south of the round retain lots of local character. Higher up, it's rough grazing, heather and bracken bashing and often loose and shaley rock in between craggy outcrops.

The Welsh Round is unique among the Big Three for traversing through so much obvious industrial history. The south of the Round explores the vast slate quarries above Blaenau Ffestiniog. The damage wrought here is devastating and poignant, vainglorious and beautiful, like coming across the ruins of an alien civilisation. As in the best science fiction, it's rich with metaphor about the rise and fall of empire; the wanton exploitation of people and place for questionable benefit; the error of our ways. There's a reprise of this atmosphere as you climb above Llanberis through the wreckage of Dinorwig quarry. It's an eerie experience on both counts, but one that adds much to the Round.

The Paddy Buckley Round is also fairly unique in that it's possible to see the entire round from multiple points on it. Snowdon – like Nevis – follows you around, but here you can see the Carneddau and the Nantlle ridge too. It's incredibly exciting to see it all laid out, and then to approach it slowly over the following hours. It's also a joy to hear Welsh spoken so frequently – on the hill, in the café and on public transport.

Where should you start from, and which way should you go? For runners, a start and finish in Llanberis has something to commend it: Following a similar logic to an anticlockwise round on the Ramsay, it gets most of the big climbs out of the way early, saves the Snowdon leg for the grand finale and then the easier, grassy hills around Moel Ellio for tired legs. However, Paddy's preference was always to do the northern legs in the dark – reaching Snowdon for nightfall and the Glyderau by dawn – simply to avoid the crowds!

As a walker, there's nothing to stop you enjoying the Round in your own time and direction, and from a starting point of your choice. Like Paddy, I've chosen to start and finish in Capel Curig, though perhaps for different reasons. Capel Curig is more accessible, by both car and public transport, from the rest of the country than Llanberis. Beginning from there and heading in a clockwise direction also has the advantage of allowing food and fuel resupply (and a shower) in Llanberis after 3–4 days even if staying high and wild camping, which for the multiday walker means carrying less to begin with. I've also chosen to go clockwise because for backpackers carrying a load, it can be useful to work up to the bigger climbs over the course of a few days.

Route guide

LEG 1
Capel Curig to Nantmor

Distance	21.3 miles (34.2km)
Ascent	7568ft (2310m)

This is a long stage over rough and remote terrain. It includes some indistinct features and challenging navigation, but provides grandstand views across to Snowdon and involves traversing through the first of two utterly fascinating quarry areas. We finish on Cnicht, a small but very beautiful mountain with wild heathland at its foot.

From the car park at Capel Curig, head towards the road junction of the **A5** with the **A4086**. Walk downhill on the **A4086**, southwest towards Llynnau Mymbyr. The Plas y Brenin National Mountain Centre is on your left around 400m along the road. Walk through the car park to the end, and find the footbridge over the lake outflow. This feels like the real beginning of the route.

Cross the footbridge and take the path directly uphill through mixed woodland. Almost immediately, you'll meet a vehicle track, but continue across and up. At a T-junction, marked with a small numbered sign on the tree ahead of you, go right to follow the main path until a second vehicle track is meet. Go left on this for about 3m and find the footpath uphill, which runs alongside a small stream. Fill your water bottle if needed. When you reach a stile, continue on the path into clear-fell and then onto open hillside.

The clear, but sometimes rocky and boggy path continues up the NNE flank of summit number 1 – Carnedd Moel Siabod (Cairn of the Bare, Shapely Hill). There's a second stile and a smaller water source on the way up. The crags you see above you are not the summit but the northeast ridge. Runners can cut right to reach the cairn early, but it's easy enough to stick to the path, which becomes braided and faint then turns due east

to meet the ridge, before turning south again for the summit. This is the first summit on the round, replete with a triangulation point. It's a magnificent top, offering views of the Moelwyns and the Carneddau, as well as looking directly into the huge *cwm* (valley) created by Llyn Llydaw at the heart of the Snowdon massif.

Passing some interesting crags that offer good shelter if needed, descend towards the *bwlch*, or pass, with the fence on your right-hand side. This is easy going on a broad grassy ridge before the short ascent to summit 2 – Clogwyn Bwlch y Maen (possibly, Pass of the Cliff). Descend carefully through a short steep slot between the rock and the fence and continue over a junction of fences at the very boggy Bwlch Rhi'r y chen. This pass offers an easy bail point to lower ground in bad weather, if necessary. Weave up through the interesting crags of summit number 3 – Carnedd Y Cribau (Cairn of the Ridge) to find a path and a stile. Keep left of the fence to reach the summit, which offers fantastic views of the lake below, the **Llynnau Diwaunedd** (Lynnau Diwaunydd on the Harvey's map).

The next section will take longer than you'd like and will be easier in clear weather. From the top, descend on rough ground. Initially, handrail the fence but when it becomes too tricky, there are numerous wide gullies off to the east that enable a less rocky, but more tussocky descent to the second pass of the day, where more bog awaits. This offers a clear path west, down to a campsite at **Llyn Gwynant**, perhaps a more useful option for walkers in bad weather. The path is marked by an attractive old gate. Go past this and ascend very soggy ground, to find a good path on the right-hand side of the fence. You can reach summit 4 – Cerrig Cochion (Brownstones) – without much of a detour.

The path is continuously interspersed with deep bogs until the beautiful fifth summit – Moel Meirch (Hill of the Ponies). After this, the going gets easier. Runners may want to approach this top directly, but for walkers it's preferable to remain on the path, which stays right of the fence, passes two more stiles, then tucks in to the left of the summit. Walk as if to pass the top, then ascend on its south side, where there are a

number of easy routes. Then continue on the path to tranquil **Llyn Edno**.

From here, runners will cut across undulating ground south of the lake to the broad top of Ysgafell Wen (White Ledge); walkers will find it simpler to use the trod near the fence, which again brings you adjacent to the summit. The ground is knolly and interesting but would be confusing in poor weather.

Pass the lovely constellation of pools near summit number 7 – Mynydd Llynau yr Cwn (Mountain of the Valley Lake) – then aim for unnamed summit number 8 ('three tops') (marked 669m on older OS maps and 672m on Harveys). It has a huge cairn perched on top, easily seen from a distance. There are lovely views from here across to the next section of the Round, to the Moelwyns and Cnicht. Descend over the back of this top and rejoin the fence for a short distance to a small lake and a junction of paths linking this pass with Cnicht.

Go straight over the main trail and continue on the trod following the fence, which turns east with the fence as the gradient eases. From here the ground appears complicated but the way through is relatively clear – just continue to follow the fence. Weave between crags and down past the atmospheric Llyn Coch before stepping over a low electric fence to climb up to summit 9 – Moel Druman (probably, Bare Hillock). From the top, there's a clear and obvious path that hugs the ridge north of the shapely **Llyn Conglog**. It's a grassy, easygoing ridge to spine-like summit number 10 – **Allt Fawr** (Big Hill) – with vast, derelict mine complexes deep in the valleys both in front of and behind you.

Coming off, it's straightforward to follow the broad ridge, staying west and then south of Llyn Conglog, over a few tussocks to meet the loch at its outflow, where it's an easy ford. Runners may choose to hug the edge of the Cwmorthin basin and make a beeline for a diagonal line down through the crags to the quarry ruins. For walkers I recommend heading over easy ground towards the old dam and outflow of Llyn Cwm Corsiog, in order to avoid getting cragbound – that diagonal is easy to miss, especially in poor weather. Cross the Corsiog outflow and refresh your bottle, then very loosely handrail the stream down across boggy ground. You should join the trod from Llyn yr Adar, a walker's option for the mountain of Cnicht. Avoid the crags where the stream

and follow it 'around the corner' to a rocky spur. Descend this to cross the stream once more, just above another waterfall, and then cross open ground to the **quarry ruins of Rhosydd**.

Aim for the slate ramp to the left of an enormous slate heap. You'll pass close by the edge of a small artificial pool ringed by rushes. At the top of the first ramp, where it meets another derelict building, bear left and leaving the 'road' ascend through hillocks to summit 11 – Foel Dhu (Dark Bald Hill). This becomes very steep, but is grassy and straightforward. It's easy going from here to follow the ridge south to the next summit. On the map Foel Dhu and summit number 12 – Moel yr hydd (Hill of the Stag) – seem like outliers, but on the ground Buckley's logic rings true, and they offer incredible views of Siabod and Snowdon to the north and west.

More grey slate than red brick

Most of Rhosydd's 200 miners lived on site between Monday and Saturday, and conditions were infamously damp, dirty and overcrowded. You can see the ruins of the barracks clearly on level 9. The men washed in the stream, brought in their own food and coal and slept on lice-infested straw mattresses, but were required to pay between 1 and 3 pennies rent a week for the privilege. Visiting medical officers regularly condemned the facilities. Working conditions weren't much better – the men walked into and out of the mines using the same ramps and tunnels as the trams used to carry the rock out. Mining was by candlelight, and the average lifespan of a Ffestiniog quarryman in the mid 1800s was 44 years. However, Rhosydd had a better reputation for safety than its neighbour Cwmorthin, known locally as 'the slaughterhouse'.

Perhaps because of these hardships, quarrymen's biographies describe a rich cultural life. Rhosydd had an award-winning choir, and the men wrote poetry and held political and religious meetings in the Welsh tradition of the Eisteddfod – a gathering of song, literature and performance. In some of these histories, the barracks are described as 'a university', but not one that most modern students would recognise.

The ruins of Rhosydd

The Rhosydd mine works, hanging high above Blaenau Ffestiniog, produced approximately 200 million slates over 80 years beginning in the 1830s. Over the course of its life, it developed into 14 floors with more than 170 chambers, most of which are now flooded. The most obvious and extensive surface ruins are on what was level 9, which at its height contained 30 saw tables and dressing machines to finish the raw rock into usable slates. There are an estimated 2 million tons of spoil laying on the surface – huge mountains of the stuff. The ownership of Rhosydd passed through various hands and the mine workings expanded opportunistically until they butted up to the neighbouring mines. There was an underground route through to Croesor quarry, which men used to escape their shift early or visit the smithy, who was better than the man at Rhosydd. Modern cavers describe this route via a 'bridge o' doom' as 'a chamber of horrors' and 'like being in Tomb Raider'!

Old quarrymen's housing at Rhosydd

Descend on grassy slopes from the flat top of Moel yr hydd, following a westerly spur, which meets a fence to the pass. The pass is marked with a red sign, warning of the danger of the mines. Here, go left through a small gate and past a cairn over the col to join a wonderful quarryman's track high above the pump storage reservoir of Llyn Stwlan, the first of its kind in the UK. This takes you easily to the col between Moelwyn Bach and Craig Ysgafn. There is flat ground here for camping, but the nearest water is provided by a stream that feeds into Llyn Stwlan. This can be accessed by following one of two paths that run on the east side of Moelwyn Bach and then dropping down to retrieve water. The path to take for water is the level one that almost immediately meets the remains of a circular building.

To ascend summit 13 – Moelwyn Bach (Little White Hill) – take the second easterly trail, which climbs diagonally up the mountain. From this, the most southerly hill in the Round, there are keystone views across the sea and over the Round. Retrace your steps, pick up your bag and climb the impressive path of summit 14 – Craig Ysgafn (Gentle Rock). This is a beautiful mountain, with its trademark quartz stripe high on the face. Occasional handholds are useful but it is sub grade 1 scrambling territory.

Descending slightly through interesting knolls, it's then a plod up a zigzag path to the broad grassy summit of Moelwyn Mawr (Big White Hill). Moelwyn Mawr has two spurs. Descend on the north easterly spur, following a clear path, before cutting north slightly to find the runner's trod, which carries you east of Llyn Croesor (which cannot be seen from the summit). Descend between gentle knolls over boggy ground to cross a flattened area and meet a quarry track leading out west of the ruins visited earlier. Flowing water can be found just south of the last building at the edge of the ruins.

Industrial heritage on the descent from Cnicht

From here, there are two options. Walkers might choose to head east on the track back into the ruins, and take the path that you took down into the area earlier. Head back up, but this time, keep Llyn Cwm Corsiog to your right. Follow the path north until just after it crosses the Afon Cwm-y-foel, then turn west and then southwest to join the main walker's path to Cnicht. This route is the dashed line marked 'walker's option' on the map.

Runners and lightweight backpackers might instead opt to head across the track and over mixed ground to join a trod that passes on the south side of Llynnau Diffwys and crosses the dam wall of Llyn Cwm-y-foel. The trod is faint, but navigation is simple in fair weather. Cross the dam and climb steeply to meet a small climber's howff, and a drystone wall a few metres away on your right. Handrail the wall steeply until it turns left a little. You'll see two crags ahead – go between them, on steeper grassy terraces until 'topping out' on a flattish ledge. Ascend diagonally on slate scree, and then head straight up to join the summit ridge. With a lightweight backpack in fair weather, this takes me around 40 minutes.

Summit number 16 – Cnicht (Knight) – is not tall, but is a spectacular mountain. Descend the steep southwesterly ridge. Where the path splits above a crag, it's easier to go left. Further down, the path drops under another crag and meets a stile. Cross the stile and head off the ridge on grasslands towards Croesor. At a gate and a signpost, instead of heading into **Croesor** itself, turn right and head in a northwest direction on an ancient and beautiful track that winds its way through heather, bracken, crags and waterfalls towards the road at **Bwlch Gwernog**. The next

stage of the Round – from Moel Hebog to the Nantlle ridge and Y Garn – lies directly ahead of you. Upon meeting the road, cross it and go straight on, over the Afon Nantmor on a quiet and winding road into the village of Nantmor.

Nantmor is a pretty, but sleepy suburb of Beddgelert – there are no shops or pub here, and runner's support should be arranged for the car park on the western edge of the settlement.

Climbing out of Nantmor, looking back to Snowdon

LEG 2

Nantmor to Pont Cae'r Gors

Distance	9.7 miles (15.6km)
Ascent	5275ft or (1610m)

This is a shorter stage over sometimes rough and unpathed terrain, in a remote part of the National Park. A sense of quiet, and extensive views to the sea more than make up for any lack of rocky grandeur, until the final scramble above Beddgelert forest, when we are treated to plenty of both.

Descending from Moel Hebog as the cloud lifts

From Nantmor, walk through the village until you meet the **A4085**, and turn right towards Beddgelert. Cross the Aberglaslyn Bridge and turn left onto the A498 towards Porthmadog. Turn the first corner on the road, and look for path on the right-hand side of the road, marked with a small National Trust sign for the Coed Aberglaslyn. If you pass the 'coach house' with a huge three-stemmed tree stump, you've gone too far! Ascend in shade to a junction with a bridge over a stream. Go over the bridge (the left fork) and either follow a deeply set zigzag path lined with moss covered stone walls, or simply handrail the stream on a path that comes and goes. The army use these woods for drills and you'll note some of the trees are equipped with bike reflectors. Near the top there is a wooden open shelter and a fire pit, which maybe useful in bad weather (if not full of squaddies or students). At a stile above and to the left of the hut, cross the stone wall, which marks the forest boundary, and follow the path onto the open hillside.

A luxury doss in the woods?

For those staying over in the woods, there's also a wooden hut/open shelter at approximately SH 589 462. Follow the edge of the forest around to the north, cross the stream and go back into the woods, following vague trods and paths near the top boundary. The ground crosses another much smaller stream and then rises. The hut is not locked and provides excellent accommodation (if not full of Army officers!), plus a firepit and some flat ground nearby for camping.

Poets and pacifists

The house at Oerddwr was a poet's refuge. As well as being home to William Francis Hughes, it was an important bolthole for his much more famous cousin – Thomas Parry Williams. Thomas was a celebrated and well-published Welsh language poet who won the National Eisteddfod many times over. He was a conscientious objector during the World War 1, publishing his poetry in pacifist student journals until they were shut down by the authorities. He became increasingly reclusive and spent much time hiding away in the house with his cousin. After the war, plans to make him Professor of Welsh were met with fierce opposition on the back of his pacifist position. He initially withdrew, before being appointed two years later.

Once on open ground, runners will cross a dry-stone wall on a soggy trod, then handrail it (about 30m away on your left) and circle around a few trees and small rocky outcrops to find the path leading right towards a farm building at SH 585 459. This is the protected birthplace and home of the Shepherd poet William Francis Hughes, aka Wil Oerddwr. It occupies a spectacular position but sadly is not open to the public. Don't try to make straight for it, especially late in the season when the bracken is high – it's quite complicated and not using a sheep/cattle trod will be slow going.

From the back of the farmstead, the track continues north for a few metres before winding west over more open ground to the right of a small stream which feeds the farmhouse. It's increasingly steep ground, of bog, grass and bracken, but the rock outcrops thin out. Cross a T-junction in the wall at approximately SH 579 457, and then head straight up the side of the grassy, blaeberry-covered slope to summit 17 – **Bryn Banog** (probably, Horned Hill). Beware, this is an unnamed hill on older versions of the OS map.

Walkers may prefer to follow the just-as-soggy but more pronounced trod to join a path, following the same drystone wall, but keeping it on your right instead of your left. This takes you to the *bwlch* between Bryn Banog and Moel ddu, the hill to your left and the first on the ridge. Moel ddu is a shapely hill, but is not on the Round! However, following the wall in this way means navigation and the ground underfoot are easier, and it avoids any risk of unsightly scars on the broadside of Bryn Banog. The extra distance is negligible. Once near the *bwlch*, you may need to cross the

wall, around SH 577 452. It's easier to do this earlier than later, as there is barbed wire where the two walls meet. Ascend a narrow ridge, again following the line of the wall. More quarry desolation can be seen behind you to the southwest, hanging above the dammed Llyn Cwmystradllyn.

Once on top, the hill broadens out. Meet the small summit cairn, leave the wall to stay on the northerly ridgeline for a short while, before descending left over easy ground to the next col, where water can be collected at approximately SH 573 458.

Stay on the west side of the col and cross boggy ground to find a good sheep trod that weaves in and out of small hillocks and crags. You'll meet a couple of small pools at the foot of the climb to summit number 18 – **Moel Hebog** (Bare Hill of the Hawk). Go up steeply in a tussocky green gully between two ill-defined ribs or crags. It has obvious footholds and is plainly used more by sheep than humans. The upper stretch switches back and forth before the ground levels out. Go right, NNW, following vague trods to reach a cairn, then a short wall/shelter and finally a wall corner, the summit trig, as well as two large guidance cairns off to the right (for the main path to/from Beddgelert).

The next section is simple, both on the knees and navigationally. Follow the wall NW downhill to the col, first on grass but with a clear path soon emerging, tightly handrailing the wall all the way down. A trickle of water in the lower reaches, and flat ground amongst craggy knolls makes this an atmospheric place to camp.

Continue alongside the wall, up through what Bob Graham Club member Bob Wightman, calls a 'curious slot', which describes this ravine in miniature just perfectly – there's nothing quite like it anywhere else on the Rounds. There are small pools and some wooden duckboards over them, just the other side.

Pick your way up the next crag, following a clear path up through grassy terraces, which ends in a very short scree chute near the first of two tops. The second of these is summit 19 – Moel yr Ogof (Hill of the Cave). Its name refers to a cave on the eastern cliffs of the hill, where the last native Welshman to hold the title Prince of Wales, Owain Glyndŵr, is said to have hid after his revolt against English rule failed. There's an old asbestos mine near the same site.

Come off to the west on a trod that becomes clearer through some rocks and then goes over a stile. Join easier, grassy ground on a very broad ridge with good, open views in all directions.

The path splits as it rises. Take the right-hand fork for rocky summit number 20 – Moel Lefn (Polished Hill). Come off this top due NNW, rejoin the path to the left of the broad ridge and then drop off steeply NE on a clear path which then switchbacks down past cliffs and crags. Lower down to the east of Cwm Trwsgl, it plateaus out. Follow a thinning path through heather and outcrops to the corner of the forest in front of you, which is marked by a slate wall, a huge hole (a slate cut/mine) and a fence.

Go over a small stile and follow the forest wall to your immediate right on a very clear path to reach a flat, boggy area. There's another stile half hidden in the trees to your right, and the wall ahead is partially collapsed. The next section to Y Gryn is tough going – the nearest translation I can find for the name is 'The Considerable' which does describe the effort you will need to make! Head N up Y Gryn over very heathery, rocky and pathless ground, keeping the fence on your left. There are

'The curious slot' before Moel yr Ogof

Looking back to the complex ground between Moel Lefn and Y Gyrn

places where the wall stops at a crag – go around to the right in each case. Handholds are useful occasionally, but it becomes easier higher up. Near the top, the wall ends in a crag and turns 90 degrees west. Again, cut right and up to the relatively small but hard-won summit number 21 – Y Gryn (possibly, The Considerable).

Descend from the unmarked top carefully, first heading NNW along the ridge of the hill. Find a trod, pass a white fence post. Runners sometimes use a short but very steep gully on the NW side at approximately SH 553 502 to exit the ridge. Look for a conifer tree below right and the old slate mine track to the left. It's not a comfortable option with a backpack, so walkers may be just as well to pursue the ridge a little further and come off the nose just to the right of the *bwlch* stone wall at around SH 553 503, and then cut back just a few metres on the path, to cross the *bwlch* by the wall.

Walkers will cross the boggy Bwlch-y-ddwy-elor and ascend on the path. Runners may have already cut the corner on the next top to tick – Mynydd y Ddwy Elor (Mountain of the Two Biers, perhaps referring to a coffin road at the *bwlch*) – by heading west on a direct line, in order to bypass a small dip on the way up otherwise. Either way, there's not much in it – and this top is

only a minute or two out and back from the path anyway.

Mynydd y Ddwy Elor

Mynydd y Ddwy Elor – why bother? You may be wondering why such a tiny blimp on the ground requires a tick on the Round. Paddy explained that when he was constructing the Round in the late 1970s, he was still using the old 1-inch maps, which showed a trig point on this summit. The trig has gone now, but there's still an old pile of rocks remaining.

The ground ahead undulates for a short while before settling down to a broad, grassy and increasingly steep spur NW leading to summit 23 – Trum y Ddysgl (Acquirer of the Ridge). At one point the path drops to the right of the ridge, then regains it. Follow it all the way up. The top section is very steep and mostly grass, which can be slippery in the wet. A tiny cairn is reached as you top out at 703m, although it's actually higher (709m) at its eastern end. Paddy regards the 709m spot height as the official summit. After ticking the 'real' summit, cut steeply down with ground

The author on Trum y Ddysgi

falling away dramatically either side of you. It feels fairly exposed at the eastern end and is quite eroded, but is not technical. Don't follow the shortcut, which drops off to the meet the *bwlch* in the east, because you will miss the official summit that way. You'd also miss an incredible view of the cliffs of Nantlle ridge, with the backdrop of Snowdon.

From the *bwlch* on the ridge, contour around and up over the rough, braided path to summit number 24 – **Mynydd Drws-y-Coed** (Mountain of the Door to the Wood). You'll reach it just a fraction before a stile and fence. The main section of the Nantlle ridge begins just beyond this. Pole and camera users may wish to stow both for this blocky grade 1 scramble. In the wet and in descent, it's more serious than its grade suggests, and caution is advised especially when carrying a backpack.

At the foot of the jumble of rocks that makes up the ridge, follow the wall until you see a breach. Cross the wall and continue N heading for an eponymous huge pile of stones, to reaching summit 25 – **Y Garn** (unsurprisingly, The Heap of Stones, or The Cairn).

To descend, go back over the wall, this time using the stile, and follow the main path down towards the car park near **Rhyd Ddu** – but only for a short while. (Note: leg 3 details route options to Rhyd Ddu – there is accommodation there). Not long after a short section of small stones underfoot, the main path begins to eer left. Look for a small trod on your right, to the SE, and head down on open ground. Where this steepens, cut further right for a few metres before heading down to meet the stream around SH 557 517. It's a good place to refill your bottle, as there's not much water to be had once in the forest.

Cross the stream and continue south to join a good, gated path leading into **Beddgelert Forest**. This is plantation forestry, but has good paths throughout. Take the first left onto vehicle track, and ignore all other turnings until you reach the level crossing at **Pont Cae'r Gors**. There is water, as well as a few perfunctory bivi spots in the woods near the layby just south of the level crossing, if you're pushed!

LEG 3

Pont Cae'r Gors to Llanberis

Distance	11.8 miles (19km)
Ascent	6217ft (1900m)

This is a relatively short and straightforward stage, the main objective being Snowdon in the middle. Going clockwise, you meet more mining archaeology before a long and lovely ridge approach to Wales' highest hill. The ground thereafter, into Llanberis, is more rolling and easier underfoot.

Just beyond the level crossing, turn right at the road for a few metres, and then left onto the Cae'r Gors farm track. In the past, runners have continued to the farmhouse on the track, then cut around the building to go up through the fields at the back to gain the summit of Craig Wen. Be aware that this is not at all popular with the farm, which has had its holiday trade affected and dry-stone walls needing repair. Please maintain the good reputation of the Round and avoid upsetting the landowner.

A few alternatives are possible. The first is to descend from Y Garn via the main path E to the Rhyd Ddu car park, either continuing E on the track towards Bwlch Cwm Llan before bearing SSE across open ground after a while towards Craig Wen, or heading S on a new (and swift) bridleway W of Llyn y Gader.

The second option stays a lot closer to the original route: Arriving at the Cae'r Gors farm track, go through the first gate, and then over a second gate immediately on your right. Cut across open access land south of the farm to meet the wall running to summit number 26 – Craig Wen (White, or Blessed Rock). Aim for the trees, a short distance to your left, and keep that wall on your left as you ascend. This diminutive hill is the gift that keeps on giving – it's ill-defined and set back a good 2km from the road. It's also one of

the quiet joys of the Round (at least once you're on it), and a superb vantage point once achieved.

From here, head NE on much easier ground, following the fence and then just fence posts all the way to the top of the iconic and easily identifiable summit number 27 – Yr Aran (The Peak). The path from the top heads NE, then N to join the quarry ruins at Bwlch Cwm Llan. Pooled water and slate spoils make an atmospheric place to camp. Follow the wall steeply down to the col, and where the wall ends, turn left to head up the south ridge of Snowdon.

Head towards the ruins for a very short time, fork right around a slate cut and go up and almost back on yourself to find a wall. Breach this and go left on a good, clear path with slate steps. Higher up there's a large fan of rock to negotiate, which requires handholds, but it's very straightforward. Above this, meet the col and the Rhyd Ddu path, just before passing summit number 28 – Cribau Tregalan (Tregalan's Ridge) – which barely registers as a distinct top.

At this point the ridge thins, but it's a simple and atmospheric route winding in and out of the crags to the top of Wales' highest mountain – summit 29, Yr Wyddfa (Snowdon). You'll reach the café first – the huge summit cairn, usually adorned with hundreds of day-trippers, is just around the back. Carbs, caffeine or something stronger, as well as toilets and drinking water can be negotiated alongside the crowds inside the café, if you arrive in daylight hours.

From the summit, follow the main path (and railway line) NNW around to the headstone above Cwm Glas. When the path splits, veer right, NE to the cairn at summit 30 – Crib y Ddysgl (Ridge of the Dish). From here, descend WNW over open ground of rock and grass, but take care not to stray too far north. Enjoy the spectacular, expansive views from here, as well as being away from the throng once more. Cross parallel to the train line and the path from Llanberis and join the rough but very clear Snowdon Ranger's path heading down the westerly spur of Snowdon.

The final section into Llanberis is a lot more straightforward underfoot. For those not on the clock, water and camp can be had at Llyn-Ffynnon-y-gwas, (a stream flows into its NW end).

Otherwise, take a right turn at SH 591 557 and follow the fence, keeping it on your right. There's a clear trod to the next objective, summit 31 – Moel Cynghorion (the Hill of the Councillors). Go over the stile where the fence meets in a V and then onto the summit, after which you need to turn left (SW) and follow the fence again to the *bwlch* before Foel Goch. Grazed grass provides swift, easy passage. The *bwlch* is a four-way junction. Turn right through a gate, ignore a stile, and take the left fork diagonally NNW, which is steeper than it looks and a little eroded near the end.

Top out to summit number 32 – Foel Goch (Red Hill). Cross at the stile and follow the fence W on a clear trod until the fence line turns left. Ignore this and continue W, dropping height

rather annoyingly before the next gentle climb via a small dogleg to avoid a crag, to summit 33 – Foel Gron (Round Hill). Continue in much the same vein on the grassy ascent of summit 34 – Moel Eilio (Elio's Hill) – crossing a couple of stiles on the way.

From the summit stone shelter, handrail the fence NE towards Llanberis. There's a path close to the fence line, although runners (and others) may wish to stay on the grass for an easier time on the knees. At the end of this long ridge, the hill steepens considerably. It's best not to continue on the path, which becomes very rough and loses height fast. Instead, come off the NE side, off trail, through gorse, hawthorn, ferns and rabbit droppings. Head for a gate with a stile to its right, onto

'I do the Snowdon 10K every year. This is just my regular training run. I don't think I'm fit enough for the Paddy' – a runner on Snowdon's south ridge

Open cast terraforming above Llanberis

a metalled road and opposite a house, at around SH 572 590. Cross a very boggy area.

Exit onto the metalled road, and ignoring the green lane to your left, head NNE through another gate on a metalled road towards the town. Pass the same house on your right (there's also a treehouse). Backpackers may wish to follow this directly to the campsite and thereafter the town, to find rest and refreshment.

For the runners, look for a kink in the road shortly after the house, with a ruined building on the right-hand side of the road. Go through a breach in the wall and head for a pedestrian swing gate on the far side of the field. Go through this and keep left of a small stream for approximately 30m to reach a green lane, with a yellow trail marker. Go down this, past a wooden house on your left to find another swing gate and a tarmacked road. Follow this ENE, and shortly after joining another track coming in from the right. Continue on alongside the Snowdon Mountain railway track and past Llanberis Falls.

You'll meet a cattle grid and a T-junction. Turn right, then left shortly after, passing a park with children's play area and into a small, suburban estate. Follow the road around – left, right, left, left, right to emerge onto the main road that runs through the town. Cross over and take the footpath directly in front of you. It has a large red 'Croeso/Welcome' sign for the **Llanberis** lake railway overhead.

LEG 4

Llanberis to Ogwen YHA

Distance	9.5 miles (15.3km)
Ascent	5711ft (1740m)

This is possibly the roughest single stage underfoot, though by no means the longest, across highly dramatic, rock strewn landscapes. It begins with complex micro navigation through the quarry.

From the entrance to the Llanberis railway, use the railway track heading NE as a handrail and cross the head of Llyn Padarn and exit at the gates. Turn right and head SE along the road for a short distance, through some ornate gates which mark the entrance to the Padarn country park. Note the road coming in from the right, and enter the power station grounds. Take the footpath on the left, known as 'the zigzags', and marked with a safety notice. This is a slate walkway, which begins up through the spoils, then diverts through some woods to reach **Dinorwig quarry**. It's a fascinating and eerie place.

Take the simple walled path, and then through the woods, where occasional handholds are useful. This leads to a flattened area. Go over a small wrought iron footbridge, with a tram winding shed on your below left. Immediately after crossing the footbridge, drop down to the right, to the level of the shed. Head SE for around 500m, as the tramlines contour left around the hillside. Go left where the path splits at a tiny shed, following a fence on your right. Pass a barracks and go around another large winding shed to the left. Continue left and then up again to a much larger, flatter area with the largest buildings in the works, on your left. Go through two swing gates and go

The start of the Foxes Path

over a padlocked gate to reach the foot of a huge incline (decommissioned concrete cable covers, marked with high voltage signs). Note that you are now off the designated footpath and further passage is entirely at your own risk. It is a mobile environment so your discretion is advised!

Many runners continue all the way up a series of these inclines, to cross an access road far above and head directly up onto the next summit, but my preference is to follow the original route as closely as possible. In this case, making use of what the quarrymen called 'the Foxes Path', which winds up through the terraces to the south of the main cutting. Go up the incline marked high voltage for 20–30m, then cut right onto a 'level' along to a flat area with three shafts cut horizontally into the hillside. At this point, the old coffin road from Nant Peris cuts across the quarry. Go up steps next to a large slate wall and into a vast open cutting, with a small arch (or tunnel) on the left. The left-hand wall is especially popular with climbers. Go to the right again, past another building and up a long flight of steps flanked by broken iron railings and a rusty pipe. Top out to another set of buildings, the largest of which

Relics inside the Caban, Dinorwig

contains quarrymen's relics, a stove and much graffiti. This was the *caban*, a building where the quarrymen took their lunch and sat out the worst of the weather.

The general trend is right and up, throughout. Continue to do so, up some rotten steps to another winch house, then more steps to access each terrace. The next major level was known as 'Australia level'. Those not on the clock can detour right for a shed containing the remains of a compressor, with the motor part removed. Further along to the south there's a cutting shed, with much of the machinery still in situ.

Dinorwig quarry

Its scale is quite mindboggling, but as vast as this place is, this was the second largest slate mine in the world. At its height, it employed more than 3000 men, but the nearby Penrhyn was even larger. Production declined after about 1890 and eventually ceased in 1969. It had become very difficult and expensive to work the slate there, as previous spoils littered the site and slid into newer pits and quarry areas. You can see these everywhere as you move through, even today – not much has changed on the ground since around 1920.

As in Rhosydd, conditions were harsh and extremely dangerous, but here the quarrymen worked high in the open rather than underground, on wet and icy galleries exposed to the elements and to rockfall loosened by blasting. A crew was made of two rockmen, a splitter and a dresser, the former freeing the rock from the hillside, the splitter breaking it into more manageable sections with hammer and chisel, for the dresser to cut into slates. The crew was paid monthly by the 'bargain', measured out in 6m blocks of rock – wages were decided by how many slates they could work from each of these bargains. However, they had to be careful; over-production meant less money, not more. Crews would often reorganise distribution between them, to try and maintain wage rates and bonuses.

Slate cutting shed, Dinorwig

Follow the rusty pipe uphill to a water tank and shed, then up a slate ramp to another winch house. Cut right for a few metres to join the last ramp. This is more of a slabby staircase, very solidly built but feeling a little exposed especially at its top end, looking down and out with the entire quarry underneath your feet. The top level was called 'Abyssinia level', because it was so high that Abyssinia (modern day Ethiopia) could allegedly be seen from it!

Dead ahead should be a small, modern hut surrounded by a green wire fence, at a road end. This is marked 'Surge Shaft' on the Harvey map. Head to the left-hand corner of the fence, going steeply up on rough steps to a metal gate. Cross the road end and continue to walk up the hill with the green fence on your right. When the fence turns its corner SE, follow a rough trod that comes and goes. Head uphill, NNE, to find two smaller cairns on the way to the quartz veined small summit of Elidir Fach (Elidor the Lesser) – summit number 35.

Now head over easy ground, down slightly before the steep scree path to the western nose of the next hill. Upon topping out, clamber over a jumble of rocks for the stone shelter on summit 36 – Elidir Fawr (Elidor the Great). There are breathtaking views of the next stage, on a very Scottish feeling hill.

Go down on a clear path on the north side of the ridge on a good path to reach the rocky *bwlch* with good views. Stay left on the ridge rather than dropping E, so as to avoid losing too much height. There's a grassy slope to a stile over a fence, and then a very short distance to the stone shelter of summit 37 – Mynydd Perfedd (Gut Mountain). Once again, impressive views, this time with an aspect favouring the Carneddau.

Follow a clear path and a fence line to the SE, then go down to the *bwlch* and then up via a switchback path to summit 38 – Foel-goch (the second 'Red Hill' on the Round). The path is sadly braided, and those away from the ridge edge are slightly less eroded. At the top, cross a small stile over the fence, for the final few metres left to the summit cairn.

Now, cross back over and follow the fence line almost directly due south, thankfully not losing too much height on easy grass, before turning SE slightly for the fairly long ascent of the next hill. Go up a slate scree, switchback path for dramatic views from the summit (number 39) of Y Garn (The Cairn).

From here, head downhill SE on a good path, first hugging the ridgeline above the cwm and then peeling off across an open upland plateau towards Llyn y Cwn. In fine weather, it's difficult to imagine a more idyllic place to camp, amongst rocky knolls, under dramatic cliffs on flat grass, with plentiful water. It is an understandably popular spot for tourists too, so treat your water if taking from the outflow.

For those without time to linger, go past the N side of the *llyn* (lake), then S up the very clear but very loose stone chute towards the summit plateau of the Glyderau. There's a small spring near the bottom of this chute if you are nervous about the cleanliness of the *llyn* for drinking water (and I have seen rubbish in it). Gradually, the incline eases and large cairns appear as the path braids.

Summit 40 – Glyder Fawr (Big Mound) – is on your left, to the east, with its cairn just off a dramatic fan of rocks pointed skywards.

From here, go across rocky ground in an easterly direction, heading for the edge of the Cwm Cneifion (nameless cwm), then south of a large, flat grassy area. The path splits – take the right-hand fork (it loses a few metres of height but is swifter underfoot at the end).

Go around Castell y Gwynt on its south side, with it on your left, then pick your way up through large boulders and flat slabs to more straightforward ground, before the more rounded boulder pile of summit 41 – Glyder Fach (Small Mound).

Go ENE off the top, keeping the famous cantilever stone on your right, and another spikey fan of rock on your left. Go down immediately to the right of this fan to find a path, or follow the cairns a little further on if you miss the fan – both lead to a large cairn with a white quartz stone set in. This is the marker for both the descent gully and 'Bristly Ridge', a grade 1 scramble.

The summit of Elidir Fawr

Ogwen Valley from Y Garn

Tryfan at sunset

Our descent here is the worst on the Round – very steep, loose and slippery underfoot. It may help to stow poles or cameras. Head down a rubbishy chute to the right (E) of Bristly Ridge. Exercise caution – it's around 300m of drop so will take time, especially carrying a pack. Eventually the ground eases and the braided path curves around to the north a little to arrive at the *bwlch*, and a stone wall with a small stile.

There are a few options for Tryfan and beyond, and it's worth reading through this next section in its entirety before you decide which way to go. Tryfan is a significant challenge on a route of significant challenges, and should not be underestimated. Once again, use this book to help you, but make sure you recce the route if you are considering a run on the clock.

Backpackers can leave their bags at the **bwlch** mentioned above, and go out and back to the summit of Tryfan, as the descent route for runners is not comfortable with a pack. Handrail the stone wall up until it meets the blocks and slabs that make up the sub-grade 1 scramble ascent to summit 42 – Tryfan (Three Peaks).

Backpackers can then return to their packs, and depending on their plans for the next summit – Pen yr Ole Wen – can opt for the following: Either head down on a well-trodden path for a beautiful camp at Llyn Bochlwyd to the west, or continue for the youth hostel at Ogwen. A third and perhaps the most logical option is to locate the 'Heather Terrace' path on Tryfan's east side (labelled as such on the map), which leads down to the road. This lines you up nicely for Paddy Buckley's original way onto the Carneddau – by the east ridge ascent of Pen yr Ole Wen (labelled 'walker's option' on the map) – which is also a more manageable (and very beautiful) route with a larger pack. However, finding the Heather Terrace path in descent can be quite a challenge, especially if the cloud is down. There are good and conveniently placed campsites at both Gwern gof Uchaf and Gwern gof Isaf, on the A5 at the foot of Tryfan.

For runners, if you don't opt for the Heather Terrace path, there is another option. From the summit of Tryfan and with your back to Adam and Eve, look W to see Ogwen Cottage. Head straight down, to find a steep and very eroded gully, which leads to a good path from a grassy area at the foot of the blocks. Paddy tells how, from here, he would run underneath Milestone Buttress and then down on scree (now all run out) to the road, before turning right, not left!

In recent years, it's now more common to take the path NW to the road and along to your changeover point at Ogwen Cottage. This path is not marked on the OS but is on the Harvey map. Note that this path splits as it nears the road – the right-hand fork exits into a layby car park further E than you need. Take the left fork to stay off the road for a little longer.

LEG 5

Ogwen to Capel Curig

Distance	10.2 miles (16.4km)
Ascent	3979ft (1210m)

After a slightly more technical start, this is a high mountain traverse on relatively easy ground to finish. Note that little or no running water can be found once on the Carneddau ridge under 'normal' conditions – the route is predominantly dry.

As indicated in the previous section, the traditional way up the next top actually takes a different route to that marked on the Harvey map. I was surprised to learn that Paddy always opted for the path alongside the waterfalls of the Afon Lloer, to then head up the path on the east ridge for summit 43 – Pen yr Ole Wen (Head of the White Light). This is also preferable for those carrying more. A wild camp at Flynnon Lloer can be incorporated if desired.

However, it's become quite commonplace for runners to use the south ridge of Pen yr Ole Wen instead (see 'runner's option' on map). This becomes a scramble near the top. Those with light packs should manage fine, but it can be a struggle with a larger load. From the **youth hostel**, go N on the road, crossing the bridge over the outflow of Llyn Ogwen. Just after the bridge on the right, find a small stile dedicated to Alf Embleton. Cross this and follow the signposted path for the south ridge. This ridge seems to have a reputation for being 'a slog' but personally I think it's a wonderful way up the hill. The path cuts back and forth across the north and south side of the nose of the ridge, requiring handholds in places. At around 780m there's a very steep, rocky gully (not loose), which is the crux and makes this a scrambling route. Stow any poles and cameras for this small section. It's not exposed at the sides, but you wouldn't want to fall. I'd evaluate this (section only) as a grade 2.

Topping out from the rocky section of Pen yr Ole Wen, you are still a good way from the summit. There's a small wind shelter near here, but this is not the top! Cut E around the rocky ridgeline on a clear trod for an easier time of it, or stick

Wild pony on the Carneddau plateau

'I used to race, but not anymore. I just like being up in the mountains these days.'
A runner on Carnedd Llywelyn

to the rocks if you prefer the views. After what seems like a small eternity, the ground levels off and the blocks recede.

Who was Alf Embleton?

A key player in the Ramblers Federation, which predated the National Association, for whom he later became Honorary treasurer until 1961, and co-founder of the Ramblers Worldwide Holidays (the more commercial wing of the Ramblers Association) in 1946. Early on, Alf was a member of the Liverpool federation, and a keen popularist in the movement to improve access and activity for all in the outdoors. In his book 'Forbidden Land: the struggle for access to mountain and moorland', Tom Stephenson (himself credited with inspiring the creation of the Pennine Way) recalls how Embleton advocated strongly for open air meetings at holiday resorts like Blackpool and Southport, in order to maximise engagement on the matter of whether the federations should come together as a national body.

The tiny summit cairn is just off to the east, and offers grand vistas over most of the Round.

From here, proceed N on easier ground, around the rim of Cwm Lloer. At the jumble of rock at Carnedd Fach, the path curves E, becoming increasingly stony. The large cairn on the horizon now is not what you think it is – the shelter stone and summit cairn for summit number 44 – Carnedd Dafydd (David's Cairn) – lies a little way beyond.

Now head E on a good path, past more cairns and a grassy section. Pass two jumbles of rock on your left – it's quicker and easier to go around, not over. The broad ridge then veers N and thins for the Bwlch Cyfryw-drum. Go over two or three more rocky sections on the *bwlch*, before the final switchback stone and scree path to summit 45 – Carnedd Llywelyn (Llywelyn's Cairn). There's a shelter and summit cairn on this broad top.

Now head down, first E, then SE on a clear path and a thinning ridge towards the scrambly Bwlch Eryi Farchog. Runners needn't go over the outcrop of rock at the head of the scramble – there's a sheep trod which runs to its right, which leads directly to the start of the scramble itself, without any unnecessary ascent and descent. Stow your poles and cameras away for this short but

Pen yr Helgi Du (left) and Carnedd Llywelyn from Pen Llithrig y Wrach

technical downclimb, estimated at a very low grade 2 in decent weather, but especially tricky in the wet. I favour a line on the right, but take your pick. It's easier without a backpack, or with a partner to pass one to.

Traverse the *bwlch*, which can feel a little airy for some but is not technical underfoot, and ascend using both hands and feet over rock, grass and mud to summit number 46 – Pen yr Helgi Du (Head of the Black Hound). Again, I favour a line on the right, cutting back left onto the nose about two-thirds of the way up.

From the summit, cross a marshy area and head for the first of two cairns guiding you down ESE to a boggy col before crossing a fence at the stile. Now it's a final climb on grassy slopes to the last hill on the round. There are three or four false summits on the way. Where it levels off, follow the path right (SE) for the cairn at summit 47 – Pen Llithrig y Wrach (Slippery Peak of the Witch).

From here, the descent is a little more complicated than the map suggests. Head S to begin the ridge-edge path down, but peel off W soon after. If the weather is clear, look out for the bridge at SH 717 609 and aim off a little right of that. Find a grassy gully, which provides easiest passage

steeply down avoiding the worst of the heathery craggy terraces to the east. At the foot of this gully, there's a useful small stream from which to fill your almost certainly empty bottle.

Aim W again after the stream. Don't join a path from the lakehead on your left, but instead find a wide trod on your right, leading to a small jumble of rocks and then the bridge itself.

We're now on the home stretch! Follow a clear but very boggy path, first SE and then S for a while over flat moorlands. There are occasional duckboards and pallets to assist with the wettest sections. Go through a gate, after which the path becomes stone. Pass a small waterfall on the left to reach a fairly large farmhouse on your right. There's a junction of sorts here – don't go left, but instead go straight on, with a tree on your left, on a green lane. Follow this old lane down to the road and a gate.

Turn left to go into Capel Curig. The paths on this stretch of road are tiny or non-existent, so take care of traffic. When you reach Capel, collapse in a heap.

Well done!

Practicalities

Getting there and around

Capel Curig is on the A5 road running between Telford and Angelsey, which in turn connects to the M54 for Birmingham. From London and the south, use the M40 to get north. From the Southwest, the M5 is a better option. From the north, aim for Manchester via the M6 and then the M56, following the A55 coast road to Colwyn Bay before turning south on the A470. For a Llanberis start, continue on the A55 around to junction 11 and take the A4244.

Public transport is possible: you can travel by train from London or Manchester to Llandudno Junction, then take a local bus (X19) towards Blaenau Ffestiniog getting off at Watling Junction, just before Betws-y-coed. To get to Capel Curig or Llanberis from there, take the Snowdon Sherpa bus (S2).

Cars at the start

At Capel Curig, a vehicle could be left in the Snowdonia National Park car park behind the small parade of shops, or occasionally and only with permission, at Plas y Brenin National Mountain Centre. The Capel Curig car park is free at the moment, but the National Park is apparently considering charging in the future.

The Snowdon Sherpa

A small but excellent mountain bus service runs up the Gwynant Valley between Beddgelert, Llanberis Pass and Capel Curig, as well as connecting Llandudno, Caernarfon and Blaenau Ffestiniog, which allows walkers to connect linear routes in the National Park.

Water

The following is a summary of places where fresh water may be found to refill your bottle. These and other points are also noted in the full route notes. Be aware that this is wild water and may need treating, especially in the valleys or on popular sections of the route (see especially Snowdon, the Glyderau).

Leg 1
- Stream on the ascent of Moel Siabod.
- Standing water at Lynn Edno, Boundary ridge.
- Outflow of Llyn Cwm Corsiog, Moelwyns.
- In flow of Llyn Stwlan, (off route for runners).
- Stream near path west of Rhosydd quarry, Moelwyns.
- Stream at the foot of Cnicht, before Croesor.

Leg 2
- Bridge over stream in the Coed Aberglaslyn.
- Small stream at the house of William Oerddwr.
- Stream west of *bwlch* under Bryn Banog.
- Streams and standing water on *bwlch* north of Moel Hebog.
- Stream on descent of Y Garn, before the forest.
- Stream alongside road at Pont Cae'r Gors.

Leg 3
- Standing water north of Yr Aran, at the Bwlch Cwm Llan.
- Drinking water from the café toilets on Snowdon's summit (if open).
- Stream at Llyn-Ffynnon-y-gwas (slightly off route for runners).
- Stream on edge of Llanberis town.

Leg 4
- Quite dry until Llyn y Cwn, under Y Garn. Treat water from the outflow.
- Stream at the foot of the path to the Glyderau plateau.

Leg 5
- Predominantly dry until a good stream at the foot of a grassy gully south of Pen Llithrig y Wrach.
- Small stream as you cross the Nant Tal-y waun, SE of the same hill.

Suggested backpacker's itinerary

The beauty of wild camping is that it can happen anywhere (within reason and the law), and I am wary of supplying times, because everyone's pace is different. Overly specific information can lead some to make dangerous assumptions in the mountains. However, here is a guide that may be useful to those trying for the full Round over the course of a week.

Day 1: Capel Curig to the Moelwyns or Blaenau Ffestiniog
Day 2: The Moelwyns to Beddgelert
Day 3: Beddgelert to Pont Cae'r Gors or Rhyd Ddu
Day 4: Rhyd Du or Pont Cae'r Gors to Llanberis
Day 5: Llanberis to Ogwen YHA
Day 6: Ogwen YHA to Capel Curig

Alternative ways to complete the Paddy Buckley Round

The Paddy Buckley is unique among the Big Rounds in that it is the most easily dissected into a comfortable walking route, with accommodation available on most or all nights. Options for each stage are suggested below.

Leg 1: Capel Curig to Nantmor – the Boundary Ridge

Capel Curig to Blaenau Ffestiniog could be completed in a longish walking day from valley to valley. I'd prefer to wild camp somewhere in the Moelwyn, because the mining areas are part of what makes this Round so unique, but dropping down into the town is certainly feasible. There are plenty of places to stay (under a slate roof), eat and shop for groceries in the town.

You could also base yourself at Nant Gwynant (accommodation suggestions, below) for leg 1 and a part of leg 4. Doing this puts you in an ideal position for the 'Snowdon Horseshoe', a big, long day involving a famous and exposed grade 1 scramble (Crib Goch), which is a rite of passage in the Welsh mountains, and was also part of the original plan for the route that Paddy and friends debated at length but was eventually abandoned.

Nantmor is a pretty but sleepy suburb of Beddgelert, and there are no shops or pubs here. If you are walking and wish to refuel and refresh, the bright lights of Beddgelert await only 2km away. It's best to stay just east of the Aberglaslyn Bridge and walk along the river on the 'fisherman's path', which narrows to a bottleneck with the aid of some boards for walking, perhaps

crossing by the narrow-gauge railway bridge and visiting Gelert's grave on the way to the pub. There's even a few crafty places to bivi by the river if you are discreet and don't mind being opposite the road. In Welsh the pass is known as Bwlch y Gymwynas, which means 'gift' or 'favour' and this is certainly one of the treats you miss if you hurtle round.

Beddgelert has plenty of shops, pubs and cafés to help you on your way (or slow you down)!

Leg 2: Nantmor to Pont Cae'r Gors – the western fringes

If stopping over in Beddgelert, you'd need to retrace your steps in order to continue the Round. If you are considering this as a longer continuous walk, then I'd recommend ending this section not at Pont Cae'r Gors itself, but coming off Y Garn on the main path and finishing in Rhyd Ddu. If 'walking the line', you may want to pack two days worth of lunches out from Beddgelert, as Rhyd Ddu has pubs and a café, but no grocery store.

The village itself is a good 'base camp' for those considering the Nantlle ridge, Y Garn and the ridge south (perhaps making use of the bus mentioned above at the end of the day), and on the other side of the valley, is well placed for most of leg 3, including the western side of Snowdon.

Leg 3: Pont Cae'r Gors to Llanberis – Snowdon's high and rolling hills

This stage is also very doable in a day for most fit walkers, and there are excellent facilities in Llanberis allowing a recharge and resupply of walking and camping food. Accommodation options are suggested below, and there's a small Co-op and numerous eateries available too. I recommend Pete's Eats if you want a good Welsh breakfast!

Llanberis is a great option for those who prefer a base to explore the ridges of leg 3 and the mining areas at the beginning of leg 4 in more depth.

Leg 4: Llanberis to the Ogwen Valley – wild and rocky

This is another discrete section that could be accomplished in a single day. For those wanting to leave the camping gear at home, there are youth hostels at both ends. The campsites or YHA in the Ogwen Valley make for a great 'base camp' to explore both eastern side of leg 4 and all of leg 5, should you wish to stride out and back, from and to a single point.

Leg 5: Ogwen to Capel Curig – the quieter Carneddau

Again, this is doable in a single day, without camping – although as a rule I'd caution against rushing this trip, unless of course you are thinking about running!

Places to stay and resupply

Here are a few campsite and youth hostel locations, which may be useful if you are planning to 'section' the round or need to accommodate support teams, as well as shop information. There is more information about nearby towns and villages in the section above. The campsites in the Ogwen valley (as well as Llanberis) may be a little rustic by modern standards, but they are set in the most beautiful places and the whole area is drenched in history.

Leg 1

Near the start of the route: Capel Curig hostel. Web: www.therockshostel.com; tel: 01690 720 225; email: info@snowdoniahostel.co.uk.

Halfway along the Boundary ridge, the following options would involve you dropping off the

Looking over Ogwen towards the Carneddau

Snowdon, from Moel Siabod

Camping just off the summit of Siabod

hill (to the tune of 300m descent, and re-ascent the following day), but may be useful:

■ Llyl Gwynant Campsite. Web: www.gwynant.com

■ YHA at Nant Gwynant. Web: www.yha.org.uk/hostel/yha-snowdon-bryn-gwynant; tel: +44 345 371 9108; email: bryngwynant@yha.org.uk.

■ Pant Lleni. Very nearby is the house that Paddy used as a base to establish the route, and it's now a holiday home. Web: www.menaiholidays.co.uk/cottages/snowdonia/pantlleni

Any of these would allow access to leg 1 and a good deal of leg 4.

Leg 2

There are plenty of guesthouses and B&Bs in Blenau Ffestiniog, and good wild camping in the Moelwyns above the village.

Beddgelert has also guesthouses and B&Bs.

There's also a forest campsite north of the village on the A4085, replete with a steam railway station! Beddgelert Campsite. Web: www.beddgelertcampsite.co.uk; tel: 01766 890288.

Leg 3

For a longer stay in the area and right on the original route, search for Rhyd Dhu Holiday Cottage (ref 2008) at www.sts-holidays.co.uk; tel: 01766 770038.

The alternate ending to leg 3 takes you to Rhyd Du, probably the best option if you are wanting short-term overnight accommodation, and the Cwellyn Arms. There is a campsite nearby (real fires), and the choice of bunkhouse or a private room. Web: www.snowdoninn.co.uk; tel: 01766 890321; email: snowdoninn@aol.com.

Leg 4

There are plenty of guesthouses and B&Bs in Llanberis, and also an excellent campsite on the edge of town:

- Llwyn Celyn Bach. Web: www.campinginllanberis.com; tel: 01286 870923; email: daviesllanberis@aol.com.
- Llanberis YHA. Web: www.yha.org.uk/hostel/yha-snowdon-llanberis; tel: 01286 870 765; email: llanberis@yha.org.uk.

Leg 5

There are three options in the Ogwen Valley:

- YHA Idwal Cottage. Web: www.yha.org.uk/hostel/yha-idwal-cottage; tel: +44 345 371 9744; email: idwal@yha.org.uk.
- Camping Gwern gof Uchaf. Web: www.tryfanwales.co.uk; tel: 01690 720294. No booking required for small groups.
- Camping Gwern gof Isaf. Web: www.gwerngofisaf.co.uk; tel: 01690 720276; email: kirstywills87@gmail.com.

Support for runners

Access on the Paddy Buckley Round requires the least amount of driving of all the Big Three. The following is a list of the most commonly used spots for support vehicles supplying food, drink and pacer changes.

Leg 1 – Capel Curig

The small car park behind the parade of shops. Vehicles can be left for a few days at your own risk. It was free of charge at the time of writing but the National Park is planning to introduce a fee. There's a toilet block next to the Joe Brown outdoor store, which is closed at night and operates a 20p charge in the daytime.

Leg 2 – Nantmor

The National Trust car park on the outskirts of Nantmor, A4085. Please note that parking fees may apply and support teams are not exempt. There are no toilets.

Leg 3 – Pont Cae'r Gors

An extensive layby on the west side of the road, opposite the farm entrance. There are no toilets.

Leg 4 – Llanberis

Either of two car parks at Pentre-Castell. Charges apply in both (the westerly one is cheaper, but smaller). Both are just a few metres from the onward leg. There are no toilets at the car parks, but plenty in the town.

Leg 5 – Ogwen Valley

The pay-and-display car park next to (but separate from) the YHA is most commonly used for the Pen yr Ole Wen south ridge route, but the A5 laybys north of Tryfan are also suitable for those ascending by the east ridge. Parking fees apply in the car park, and while vehicles are not supposed to be left overnight, toilets are available 24 hours a day.

Rules for runners

The Welsh Classical Round, known also as the Paddy Buckley Round, is a little different to the other two Rounds in terms of what constitutes a successful completion. Its author insists neither on a specific direction nor on a particular starting point. It doesn't *even* need to be finished within 24 hours, although most dedicated hill runners will attempt to come within that time. Unlike the Bob Graham Round, you don't need to pre-register or have witnesses or support runners.

In Paddy's words: 'If you cheat, you are only cheating yourself.'

A finisher is classified as anyone who runs the Round in a single push, regardless of his or her time. That doesn't mean backpacking attempts, though! Food and clothing caches are also acceptable, if attempting the Round without support on the ground.

In common with all of the rounds, Paddy likes to see a written report of the attempt. Like Charlie Ramsay for his Round, it is Paddy who currently keeps the records of successful completions of the Paddy Buckley Round. His contact email is buckleypaddy09@gmail.com. You should include your full name, your finish time and the dates you ran, where you started from and at what time you commenced. A trip report and a schedule is also useful for verification purposes.

The history of the Round

I can do no better here than quote (with permission) from Paddy Buckley's own account: A long day in Snowdonia – notes on the setting up of the Welsh 24 Hour Round, which was first published in Compass Sport in February/March 1983. Wendy Dodds (the first person to complete the round) also tells the story of the run itself.

By the end of 1982, 239 men and five women had successfully followed in Bob Graham's footsteps, although only a handful of these have sought to increase the tally of peaks beyond 42. Despite this prodigious depth of talent, no one until 1980 had attempted a similar 24-hour round in Snowdonia.

There had been a scattering of notable long walks over the hills of North Wales. The Rucksack Club had shown the way: Barmouth to Aber, over the hills, is a regular in the club's calendar. At different times, Stan Bradshaw, Peter Dawes and Jim Loxham have each attempted to get round all the peaks over 2500ft in Snowdonia in one continuous run. In June 1976 two members of the Long Distance Walkers Association, Neville Tandy and Chris Winn, made a double traverse of the 14 3000ft peaks but they took more than 34 hours, a very leisurely pace.

There was indeed a club, the Mad Hatters, founded by the Rev. Peter Travis, which offered certificates to those who have completed the double traverse within 24 hours. On 17–18 June 1978, John Wagstaff of Tipton Harriers went one better and did a triple crossing in 22hr 49min, a powerful if unimaginative performance. The distance involved was about 63 miles with around 27,000ft of ascent, an effort equivalent to a Bob Graham Round in terms of physical achievement. Aesthetically however, there is no comparison. The Lakeland 42 is a lovely course, flowing and logical, with shape and purpose and ever-changing horizons.

The author (David, not Paddy!) attempts to find his feet on the Glyderau

A Welsh Round should have these same qualities. The line or the shape of the round is all-important. It must remain fluent and uncontrived; dog legs, crossovers and repeated sections should be avoided. (Our modern Steeple was probably not included by Bob Graham: Looking Stead certainly was, but he forgot to record his time there.)

In addition, the Round should be the region's showpiece, giving variety and interest. Because of the large expanse of the Lakeland fells, the Bob Graham Round is inevitably selective; several areas remain unvisited and several tops of more than 2500ft are neglected. Snowdonia in contrast is a more compact area. So here it was sensible to stipulate that the Round should link up all the main groups of hills: Moelwynion, Eifionydd, Snowdon, the Glyderau and the Carneddau. It was also prudent to exclude Mynydd Mawr because of the very sensitive problems of access in 1978.

"The line or the shape of the round is all-important. It must remain fluent and uncontrived; dog legs, crossovers and repeated sections should be avoided."

In Lakeland, there are only four tops over 3000ft; in Snowdonia, there are 15. Should they all be included in the Round? During the planning stages, about a dozen different courses were evaluated, varying from 38 tops to a super-round of 70 tops, which included 64 of the 69 summits in North Wales over 2000 ft. None of these satisfied all the criteria. So, some compromises were made. Heights and height differences were given a lower priority. The aim was to establish what could truly be termed a classical Round.

The seed for this project was sown in 1977. That stimulating 'Life-Enhancer' Chris Brasher had persuaded me to join him on a Bob Graham attempt. We both failed. But the bid had opened my eyes to the fact that the Round was possible, not just for supermen, but also for those ordinary mortals, who were determined enough and fit enough for the task. Snowdonia was an area that I knew very well. I was a member of a mountaineering club that had a hut there. Why not train for the Bob Graham by doing a 24-hour round in Wales? First, I needed an accurate figure for the distance covered by Bob Graham, variously reported as between 70 and 140 miles. Using the 1:25,000 map and a map-measuring wheel, I found the route, on paper, was no more than 60 miles (other sources show it to be longer).

I ran the wheel over the Snowdonia map, along a course of familiar walks. It came out as 57 miles, 43 peaks and about 26,000ft of ascent. Fascinated, I spent hours on the maps; measuring, calculating, trying variations, seeking short-cuts. Eventually I had a detailed specification for a Welsh 24-hour Round.

On 21 January 1978, I travelled up to North Wales with Chris Brasher and mentioned what I'd been doing. We stopped at Pen y Gwryd. In the Inner Sanctum were 10 of the 'hard men' of the Rucksack Club; including George Rhodes, Ted Dance, Denis Weir, Don Talbot, John Richardson and Mike Cudahy. I announced my scheme for the Round and sought to use their collective advice and experience. Two nights later, after an excellent dinner, we spread out the maps on the table at Pant Lleni, Chris Brasher's cottage above Llyn Gwynant. The Life-Enhancer, mellowed by drams of Glenmorangie, examined my round on paper. 'Can't have Crib Goch', he decreed, 'too dangerous for fell runners; might get cramp'. 'This', said he, stabbing his pipe at Moel Cynghorion, 'this is the fell runners' ridge – a classic – absolutely essential. We could then drop down to Llanberis Youth Hostel and get Joan and Denis (Glass) to provide some tea. Then straight up through the quarry to Elidir'.

I pointed out that the Central Electricity Generating Board had closed all rights of way in the quarry, including the route from Deiniolen to the church at Nant Peris, which had been used for generations by coffin bearers, and that furthermore the quarry was patrolled. 'Go through it at night,' he said, easily dismissing the vast powers assembled against us. Yr Elen was rejected as a boring deviation; Foel Fras and Foel Grach were 'piddling little bumps'. My Round was taking a hammering. I argued to retain Crib Goch but could not convince him. Far into the night, we discussed variations and laid down criteria. We totted up the summits so far agreed. Incredibly it came out as 42 tops and about 60 miles. Chris summed it up in the logbook: 'A great night's work; this looks to be a classic.'

Back at the drawing board, I tried every possible way to keep Crib Goch. But Chris was right, although for the wrong reason. The NW ridge of Snowdon, ending on Moel Eilio, was the key to the essential shape of the Round, and all subsequent attempts were based, with minor additions and variations on the route we worked out that night. There was one important proviso. 'If the Welsh Round is to have credibility,' Chris declared, 'it must first be done by someone who has also done the Bob Graham Round.'

The next task was to devise a schedule. Here, Fred Rogerson's collection of Bob Graham reports was invaluable. Using his detailed records, I worked out a variation of Naismith's Rule, which seemed to fit the sort of pace I expected to

maintain; ie (distance/4mph) plus (height/3000ft pr hr). Towards the end of April 1978, starting from Pant Lleni, I ran over both halves of the Round on two consecutive days. The schedule was about right.

The Classical Round was beginning to take shape. To enhance the aesthetic appeal, I planned to be on Snowdon at sunset and on Tryfan at dawn. At least I would miss the crowds. This involved a difficult night section, but then there was nothing anywhere as easy as Helvellyn and the Dodds. A couple of unexpected bonuses came up. The Foxes' Path, a way up through the enormous Dinorwig Quarry was a revelation. A series of steps and staircases, ramps and inclines, paths and levels, all made and placed by hand, seemed a work comparable to the building of the Pyramids. Above on the narrow crest of Elidir, we could look into Marchlyn Mawr, and observe every stage of the construction of the new pumped-storage top reservoir. At the southern

Moelwyn Mawr from Llyn Terlyn, leg 1

end of the Round our route took us along the exhilarating high-level track above Llyn Stwlan, the first pumped-storage scheme in North Wales.

Two years passed. The demands of a new job had pushed the Classical Round into the background. At intervals, however, every section was repeated in training, variations were timed, and the route was fixed indelibly in the memory. In April 1980, Ken Turner and I came down to Snowdonia for a week's special training, going over every section of the Classical Round. On 3–4 May we did the Bob Graham Round and felt so pleased with ourselves that we set 13–14 June as the date for an attempt on the Classical Round. On the day the weather was so awful that we didn't even start. We tried again on 23 August, this time bringing in Wendy Dodds, who had completed her Bob Graham Round on 21 July 1979. The weather was perfect, but the two men both ran into problems, and the attempt was abandoned halfway.

"The Foxes' Path, a way up through the enormous Dinorwig Quarry was a revelation. A series of steps and staircases, ramps and inclines, paths and levels, all made and placed by hand, seemed a work comparable to the building of the Pyramids."

I resolved to make one last effort in 1982, and became very fit. Wendy, just back from a year in New Zealand, was willing to have another go, and we set a date for 1 May. I ran the Three Peaks race as a depletion run. It was my best time ever, 3hr 45min, with Wendy just a few minutes behind. The team assembled on 30 April, and we rang the Met Office at RAF Valley. The forecast was terrible; gale force winds, heavy rain, snow above 2000ft. We decided to postpone the event, and just went out for a long run instead, in difficult conditions. The decision was wise. During the storm that night two young Scouts camping on Snowdon died of exposure.

We tried again on 29 May, with Welshman Bob Roberts along as a serious contender. The two men failed but Wendy Dodds carried on and became the first person to complete the Classical Round. Her time, including rests, was 25hr 35min. On four of the five sections, she was inside the schedule. She lost time

WENDY DODDS – IN HER OWN WORDS

I got to know Paddy via Chris Brasher and the Karrimor International Mountain Marathon (the KIMM) – now known as the Original Mountain Marathon. Paddy, myself and others spent a lot of time going over sections of the route in early 1982, including at night. Paddy knew it like the back of his hand having spent a lot of time in 1981 going over it with the late Ken Turner.

We started at 8.53am on Saturday 29 May 1982. There were three contenders on leg 1 to Aberglasyn: Paddy, myself and the late Bob Roberts, a local Welsh speaker. We began at what we came to call 'Wendy's gate'. It's the point where you join the road before Capel. We did that so we did not have to run on the road at the end. We had no donkeys or navigators, and each of us was carrying our own kit. We were met in the quarries by Ken Turner and a friend of mine, Val Steele. Paddy had arranged a bath at Aberglasyn as he had come unstuck at this point in the past. Bob and I waited patiently for 30 minutes while this happened. On the next section, I was carrying an extra litre of water for

Paddy who very quickly dropped out – in my opinion because of overheating.

Bob and I carried on over section 2 to Beddgelert Forest and then on to the Snowdon section. Bob dropped out after Snowdon. After Moel Eilio, I was told Denis Glass might come up to meet me from the youth hostel. I was pace counting in the dark but I lost concentration, so I ended up going into Llanberis and had to go back up to the hostel.

At this point, Paddy tried to persuade me to stop, but I always feel it is better to complete a challenge, no matter what the time. After that, it's just a question of speeding up, rather than worrying about whether you can do it. Ken Turner came with me for the next two sections but we misjudged our navigation early on into the quarries and ended up climbing up slag heaps. A friend had left my car at Llyn Ogwen, complete with food and fluid, so we could refuel before the Carneddau. Paddy and Bob came up to meet me again on Pen yr Helgi Du before the final run down to Capel Curig.

between midnight and dawn when after taking a wrong turn in the Quarry she became very weary.

47 tops were climbed, 10 of which are less than 2000ft and five of which have no official OS names. We christened them, where we could, in respectable Welsh, taking the advice of Emyr Hughes, a park warden, whose family had lived in Arfon for generations.

Having nominated 47 tops, I am only too conscious how critically each will now be scrutinised for validity. The Moelwynion section is particularly suspect, 'a rough backbone with bumps'. My own feeling is that I would rather be on Moel Meirch any day, than on Snowdon. The number of tops is not that important; they are merely the markers or controls that fix the route and give it its shape.

The Welsh Classical Round was always intended to be a personal challenge. As it was considered to be a good hour longer than the Bob Graham Round, one had to lift one's sights accordingly. In the Moelwynion particularly, the going is rough and the navigation much more

demanding. Consequently, the rewards are that much greater. The Round was also a celebration to mark the countless pleasures experienced in wandering these lovely Welsh hills over many years.There are other challenges, both here and in other places. We are only scratching at the surface of what is possible. No longer is the 24-hour run unknown territory. So much knowledge and experience has been passed on, particularly by members of the Bob Graham Club, that it is now a simple matter to devise your own 'long run'. All you need is a map, a knowledge of your own pace, and the knack of constructing a schedule. Having worked it all out on paper, you then put it under foot. And this is where the real interest lies, for a schedule cannot allow for cramp or fatigue or injury, or getting lost, or indeed for any of those human frailties that provide the essential personal challenge.

Only the bare bones of the course are given. It is up to you to provide the flesh and muscle and sinew.

A runner's story: Sue Walsh

Sue was only the third person to run a complete Paddy Buckley Round, in a time of 24hr 52min in May 1984. Below is the story of her moonlit round, transcribed from a handwritten account in the Pant Lleni record book, and prefaced by some fond remembrances over telephone and email.

The Paddy Buckley Round was my first and something that I will always remember. I had never done a run longer than 6 or 7 hours before; this was prior to my entries into mountain marathons. It was unusual in that it was all rather done off-the-cuff. I ended up running most of it on my own and didn't really have much support after the first section, until I met up with Paddy for the last section. The night porter at the Royal Victoria was quite astounded when I arrived in the early hours of the morning, asked him to pour out six cups of tea and then rushed off to the loo! On reappearing I downed the tea one cup after another, said goodnight and thank you, and disappeared.

Mike, who worked with Dave at Plas Y Brenin, met me at Ogwen having driven our car from Capel Curig, and he had no idea that he was supposed to 'look after me'. He sat in the driving seat while I ferreted around in the boot getting something to drink and some food! This was so different to the Bob Graham experience where you are overwhelmed with pacers, support vehicles and the like. Those contrasting experiences influenced me to be self-sufficient when I did the Joss Naylor, with only Wendy Dodds running with me and each of us carrying our own gear – although Dave and Paddy did bob up on the last section of the Naylor to run in with me. That was special.

Paddy with the Pant Lleni notebooks at his home, 2016

When I did the Tranter Round (a shorter version of the Ramsay Round) later on, I chose to do that in a similar very low-key way.

Paddy phoned: 'How about a training run over two or three sections, starting at 5ish and running on through the night, making full use of the almost full moon and the exceptionally fine weather?' Great idea – immediately followed by the thought of continuing if things are going well.

At 4.50pm on 13 May, we set off from Bwlch Gwernog under blue skies, not a cloud in sight and with a settled forecast for at least 36 hours. A wave from Dennis as we passed through Aberglaslyn and then up on to Bryn Banog and Hebog and we were really on our way. The Eifionydd section seemed to fly by and I felt great – 30 minutes up – we'll need that in the later sections. We picked up drinks at Bwlch y Ddwy Elor from Jamie, who stayed with us until we met Dave

and the boys at Pont Cae'r Gors for our scheduled rest. Paddy was having problems with his insides (8.12pm).

Onto the Snowdon section, with Paddy still having problems and looking grey, but Craig Wen and Yr Aran went well. The timing was perfect, with a blood red sunset and a huge moon and still not a cloud to be seen. We reached Bwlch Cwm Llan for dusk and Paddy decided to drop down to Pant Lleni in the Gwynant – he looked and sounded awful. I was very sorry to see him go and felt quite lonely on my own, but I steamed on. There was no need for a torch except to 'clock in' on the summits and for a short section off Crib y Ddysgl. Bright moonlight, and a warm gentle breeze. The long grassy Moel Cynghorion to Llanberis section was magical and beautiful running. Lights in the valleys on both sides of the ridge, silver streams and lakes – even the sheep had an ethereal quality!

Sue Walsh and Paddy Buckley
© Paddy Buckley Collection

Sunset at the southern end of the Paddy Buckley Round

Victoria Hotel and 40 minutes up! There were cups and cups of welcome tea from the night porter. Then I was off up through the quarry on the Foxes Path, slow and steady, absorbing the atmosphere, eerie yet exciting, winding up the stairways and passing disused buildings. Elidir Fach and Fawr followed by Perfedd and more. Some easy, some hard work – my knees were feeling sore now. Steadying off, experiencing ups and downs, good and bad patches but the sinking moon reflected in Llyn Cwn, a much-needed perk and a blood red sunrise behind the Carneddau contrasted with the mindless flog up onto the Glyderau. I lost some precious minutes, but was determined to be up on schedule by the time I reached Ogwen. But I was slow off Tryfan, down with only 7 minutes in hand (6.13am).

"Lights in the valleys on both sides of the ridge, silver streams and lakes – even the sheep had an ethereal quality!"

At this point, a 24-hour Round was looking doubtful, as there was still a long way to go. It was good to see Mike at the scheduled break – but I was feeling quite low. I foolishly didn't take enough fluid. It was hot and dusty up Pen yr Ole Wen, but I was gaining some time. The Carneddau were slow going and I found myself frustrated by my inability to make full use of the good running terrain – my progress could be best described as painful but persistent – still, I couldn't have everything on my side! I fared better on to Pen Llithrig y Wrach, and coming off I caught sight of Paddy waiting on the road. Spirits rose, and with a lump in my throat I ran into home territory and knew that I was going to make it, 24 hours or not. Now only two minutes up (10.22am).

At Plas y Brenin, it was strange to be in my own kitchen drinking tea without a thought of stopping, but it was such a good morale boost having someone to talk to. There were clean clothes, lots of liquid and good company for the last fling. I was slow up Siabod, but then gradually fell into a sedate overdrive, where I felt as if I could go on for ever. I really enjoyed myself through the rolling Boundary section, chatting and tucking in behind Paddy. It was very hot, with not much of a breeze. I was suddenly very tired and cold for Moelwyn Mawr and the last haul up Cnicht. After the summit, there was a quick grin and a handshake and then down. Sore legs and all the ups and downs pushed to the background. I enjoyed running along the track, and felt good. It wasn't 24 hours (5.42pm). But next time...

The Charlie Ramsay Round

28,879FT (8800M) OF ASCENT OVER 57.6 MILES (92.8KM),
23 MUNROS AND 1 SUBSIDIARY TOP (24 SUMMITS)

An inversion clears over the arête, from the summit of Càrn Mòr Dearg

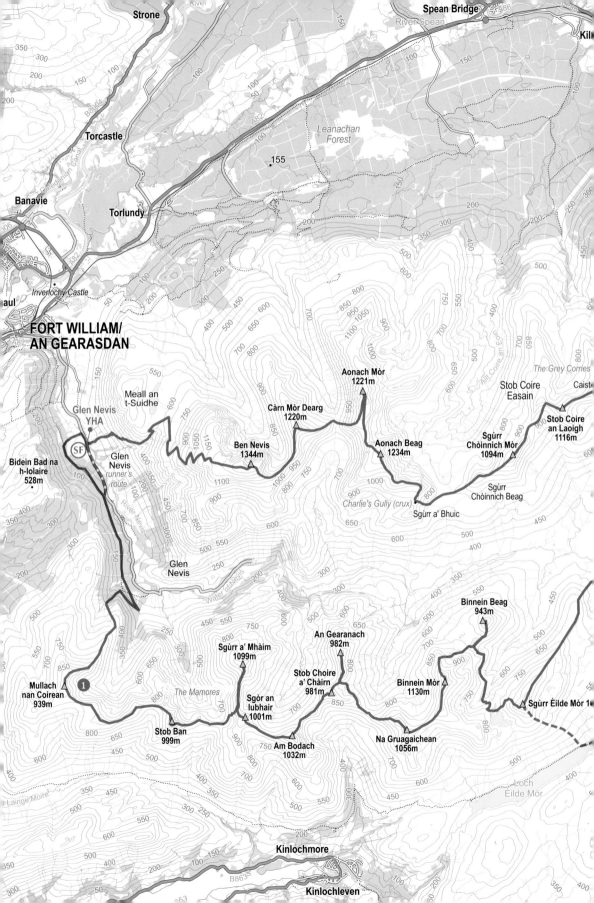

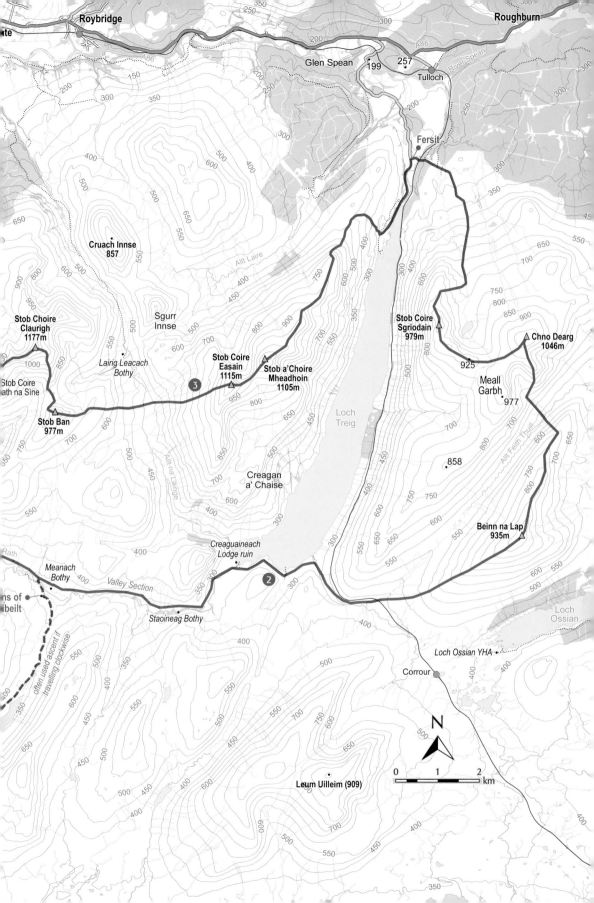

Roybridge

Roughburn

Glen Spean

199 257

Tulloch

River Spean

A86

Fersit

Cruach Innse
857

Allt Laire

Stob Choire
Claurigh
1177m

Sgurr
Innse

Stob Coire
Sgriodain
979m

Chno Dearg
1046m

925

Stob Coire
ath na Sìne

*Lairig Leacach
Bothy*

③

Stob Coire
Easain
1115m

Stob a'Choire
Mheadhoin
1105m

Meall
Garbh
977

Stob Ban
977m

Allt Feith Thuill

858

Allt na Lairige

Loch
Treig

Creagan
a' Chaise

Beinn na Lap
935m

*Creaguaineach
Lodge ruin*

Rath

*Meanach
Bothy*

②

Valley Section

Loch
Ossian

ns of
ibeilt

often used ascent if travelling clockwise

Staoineag Bothy

Loch Ossian YHA

Corrour

N

Leum Uilleim (909)

0   1   2
km

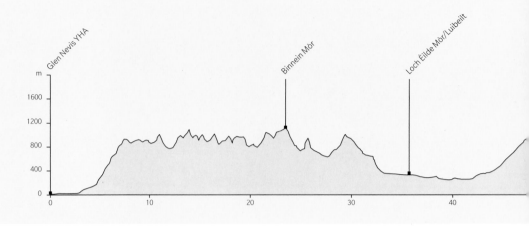

Like the Welsh Round, the Scottish Round was devised as an equivalent to the Bob Graham Round, north of the border. For much of its 57 miles, it follows challenging and exposed ridges with limited escape options. It includes a visit to mainland Britain's highest place – *Beinn Nibheis*, or Ben Nevis. It's the shortest of the three in this book, but its 24 summits offer the most ascent.

It's the only one of our three that doesn't sit within a National Park, but nearby Fort William is the second largest conurbation in the Scottish Highlands, and visitors to Ben Nevis exceed 160,000 a year. As you'd expect from a Round which only meets a main road twice (the same one, at the start and finish!), much of the route is far more difficult to access than the other two. Although the Munros (hills over 3000ft) of the Mamores and the Grey Corries are popular for day walkers, the eastern end of the Round is less frequented. In terms of feeling 'out there', the Scottish round is a league apart from the other two.

Evidence of transhumance is observable on the way – there are ruins of shielings, where herdsmen sheltered alongside cattle feeding on summer pastures. Upper Glen Nevis is still grazed in this way. There are also the remains of a lodge near Loch Treig (once the termination of a drover's road, used to transport cattle to market), and atmospheric deer stalking huts and farm buildings that have a new lease of life as bothies, which can be used for overnight shelter (though not for runner support points). Red deer partly adapted to the high ground are plentiful, especially on

the Mamores leg, but native woodland and its associated wildlife is mostly limited to Glen Nevis and around Loch Treig, largely a result of deer overgrazing.

As on the other two Rounds, the area was both highly volcanic and subsequently glaciated, with magma uplift giving literal rise to the Mamores and the Ben Nevis massif. Glen Nevis was initially formed as a result of the collapse of the crust between the two, forming a caldera. In fact, the phenomenon of 'Caldera Subsidence' was first noted by geologists in Lochaber. Volcanic magma cooled to form the red granite of the Mamores, while coastal sandstones crystallised to form the quartzite that gives the Grey Corries their name. Glaciation then went to work on the mix of rock to produce the sharp ridges, corries and U-shaped valleys we see today.

As the rock is mixed, so is the terrain. In general terms, the western end of the Mamores (notwithstanding Stob Ban) are by turns grassy, sometimes loose and crumbly, and the Grey Corries rocky and blocky. Beyond Loch Treig, the hills are more rolling, but a feeling of real remoteness coupled with the roughness underfoot can surprise the uninitiated.

This guide has chosen to go anticlockwise as championed by Charlie Ramsay in his original sub 24-hour run. As Charlie points out, this isn't the most popular for runners, as all the big climbs come at the end, when contenders are tired. A clockwise option means an easier finish on the Mamores. For backpackers, going anticlockwise

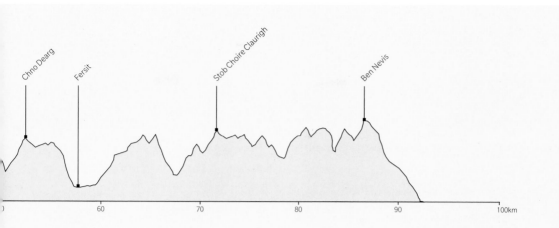

Chno Dearg
Fersit
Stob Choire Claurigh
Ben Nevis

60   70   80   90   100km

also means that finding a suitable weather window long enough to attempt those last big climbs, is another challenge to add to the considerable list already posed by the route.

Despite this, in writing the guide, I wanted to honour Charlie's original Round, which in turn pays homage to the earlier Tranter Round (see Alternative ways to complete the Charlie Ramsay Round). Both of these culminate on the UK's highest mountain, Ben Nevis, a fitting finale for the most remote of the Big Rounds. This acknowledges the historical achievements of both people, as well as the elegance of line of the original.

In 1981, Sgor an Iubhair on the Mamore Ridge acquired Munro Status, resulting in Tranter's Munro total being increased to 19 Munros and Ramsay's Munro total being increased to 24. In 1997, following a further revision of Munro's Tables, Sgorr an Iubhair was demoted and is now only recognised as a top on the main route between Sgùrr a' Mhàim and Am Bodach. Therefore, Tranter's Round includes 18 Munros and 1 Top (just as when Philip and Blythe did it), and Ramsay's Round now includes 23 Munros and 1 Top (as was the case when Charlie set his record).

Charlie is clear that the Round does not have to be completed within 24 hours. 'These notes, together with the appropriate maps and skills should enable runners and walkers to plan a route that is suitable for their own capabilities and to enjoy the round at a pace that is appropriate to them,' he says.

Backpacking the Mamores, from Stob Ban to the Devil's Ridge

119

Route guide

LEG 1

Glen Nevis to Luibeilt
via the Mamores

Distance	22.1 miles (35.6km)
Ascent	11,610ft or (3540m)

This leg involves some fiddly navigation at the start, before a long, exposed ridge at the centre of some of Scotland's finest mountain scenery, surrounded by steep drops into enormous corries. The ridge is mostly broad but there are some sections of crumbly rock and easier scrambling.

Beginning from the **Glen Nevis Youth Hostel**, runners can head south up the glen on the road for around 1km until NN 132 706, where there is a forestry ride, which allows simple access to the forestry track running parallel to the west of the road. Look for a tiny, worn trod up to the fence on your right, and a knee-high wooden marker behind. Cross the fence and head up to a second fence over grass and sorrel. Pass deadfall on your left and find the track above. It's an efficient shortcut.

The route best suited for walkers (and the one shown on the map) is to head north out of the glen, turning left just after the Glen Nevis restaurant on a tarmacked road, which in turn leads to a 'resident's only' car park and a path into Forestry Commission land. Turn left at the top of this path to gain the forestry track.

Head due SSW on the forestry track (approximately 2km for runners, 3km for walkers) until you meet a gate and a junction. Take the right-hand fork, uphill. At the time of writing, there is still a lot of forestry work happening in this area and the landscape is mobile! The forest rides (beginning around NN 137 684) that runners have traditionally used to shortcut the track switchbacks are choked with deadfall and most will now find it far easier to follow the track for another 0.5km,

and then continue on it as it switches back NNW. Ignore another junction and continue on until you reach a cleared area. Just after this, at NN 135 684, there is a flagstoned path on your left going uphill, marked with cairns on either side of the stones. Take this path through cleared forestry and then picturesque birchwood. After a short distance, you'll come to a stile over a deer fence, which leads onto the open hillside. Cross the stile and handrail the fence, going steeply uphill on boggy terraces to gain a broad ridge to the east of Coire Riabach.

Follow the clear path up the ridge, continuing to follow the fence, SSW. At the boundary end, the ridge gradually thins before becoming steeper and rockier. It's a characterful but uncomplicated beginning. The summit of the first Munro – **Mullach nan Coirean** (translated as Summit of the Corries) – is flat and littered with pink granite. Follow the corrie edge around to meet the summit cairn at 939m.

Continue around and descend SE on fast and easy grassy slopes. There's a clear path all the way along to Stob Ban, which tracks the corrie edge. At NN 136 655 the path splits to cross a crumbling red crag – both paths are viable, with the lower one slightly faster. From here, the next hill looks taller than it is. The path cuts a corner below spot height 912m before the final climb up beautiful, short but awkward veined quartz talus of Munro number 2 – **Stob Ban** (White Peak).

To descend off Stob Ban, go a few metres south of the summit cairn to find another pointed cairn, which marks a waist-high slot in the rock leading to steep and crumbling descent due east. This has suffered heavy erosion and the ground is very loose. It eases at the bottom of the slope, and the path continues through grass towards the Lochan Coire nam Miseach. This is a good place to hydrate and a popular camping spot.

From the lochan, go up the hill NE on a series of short switchbacks to reach the *bealach* (a pass or low point between two summits) before the out and back to the summit of Munro 3 – **Sgùrr a' Mhàim** (Peak of the Large Rounded Hill or Peak of the Pass) via the Devil's Ridge. If you are backpacking, this is a good place to leave bags, as the ridge can be tricky in one or two places.

Summit sunset at Mullach nan Coirean

Follow a clear path N, on the left of the ridge at first, then thinning as it reaches the crest. At the first of two more technical sections, the blocks on the crest can by bypassed by a path on either side. At the second, the slab can be bypassed by a small gully on the left, or by simply climbing down the slab following the line of the rock. This is sub grade 1 scrambling territory but is quite exposed, and more serious under snow and ice. From the foot of the second tricky section, it's a final slog to the summit, which provides a wonderful view of the whole Round. Out and back for walkers is approximately 1 hour.

Back at the *bealach*, clamber the short distance SE to the summit of Sgòr an Iubhair (Peak of the Yew). This hill was demoted by the Scottish Mountaineering Club (who look after the Munro classification tables) in 1997, so is officially no longer a Munro. However, it is very much both on the Ramsay Round and in your way, so it has to be visited! It's hardly a chore and a very nice quartzite top indeed with some fine views back over that impressive ridge you've just wandered.

From the summit cairn, go S and then SW to follow the path and descend to the bealach towards Munro 4 – Am Bodach (Father or Old Man). By this point, route finding should be fairly

straightforward, rising and falling with the ridge. Ignore the path leading south off the ridge, and another which contours through scree to the north of the summit, and head uphill E. It's a beautiful hill on ascent, first blocks and stripes of rock, interspersed with a thin, winding path to the summit cairn.

The descent is to the NE of the cairn and is steep and very loose underfoot. The way down cuts between two ribs of rock and can be awkward with a pack.

Make your way down to another col, then via a small intermediate hill, take grassy slopes to the rocky top of Munro 5 – Stob Choire a' Chàirn (Peak of the Corrie of the Cairn). From here, head north on a ridge that curves around to meet the other spur of the Ring of Steall – Munro number 6 – An Gearanach (Short Ridge, or Sad Place).

The col below this mountain is a good option for camping. There is a good source of water from a spring about 40m below the col to the SE, at NN 188 661.

To climb An Gearanach out-and-back, go up steeply following a path that winds on and off the ridgeline. Once it levels out, on the first top there are occasional sub grade 1 scrambly sections, avoided by paths to the right. After a small

On top o' the world, on Binnein Mòr

downclimb the ridge broadens for the final walk up to the summit cairn. It's not technical but a little exposed in places and best done without backpacks. Out-and-back for walkers will take approximately 50 minutes.

Return to the *bealach*, and traverse the NE flank of Stob Choire a' Chàirn by descending east to an area of drainage. An old stalker's path follows a grassy rake around the hill across often boggy ground to gain the eastern ridge of Stob Choire a' Chàirn just before the *bealach*. Continue SE to the *bealach*, ignore paths left and right, and go uphill on grass, then steeply on quartz choss for the first of the two tops making up Munro 7 – **Na Gruagaichean** (The Maidens). The first climb is tortuous despite being only approximately 250m above the *bealach*. It levels out to a short, pleasant grassy ridge. Downclimb a short but loose section of bad rock and then climb over blocky quartz for the actual Munro summit. On the map, it's easy to see this as one top, but the reality on the ground is two very distinct and separate summits (hence the reference to 'maidens').

From there, go down ENE on quartz blocks until a thinning arête, which leads to spot height 1062m. There's a slight drop before the final pull north to the summit of Munro number 8 – **Binnein Mòr** (Big Peak). Beyond the summit, there is a level ridge of approximately 50m, with large granite blocks to work over and around – again, it's not technical but it is exposed. It's one of the most dramatic situations of the whole Round, with impressive views into Coire an Easain and across to Nevis and the Aonachs.

From the end of this small ridgeline, descend due NNW, steeply at first to swing around on the northerly ridge of the corrie below. Runners may choose the corrie itself for a faster descent but it holds snow late in the season, so my advice would be to use the ridge. It's possible to drop into the corrie steeply at around 900–950m on eroded, clay-like soil (or else use the ridge to descend fully and then work around to the east). Cross the corrie, find the spring and handrail this down to the two small lochans, and later a larger lochan, at the foot of Binnein Beag.

The area under this top makes for a fine camp, with plenty of fresh water and flat pitches.

It's also possible to use the east ridge of Binnein Mòr for ascent/descent. In descent, head down to approximately NN 215 664, keeping the rocks on your left. Then head down NNE to the hanging valley of Gharbh Choire to join the waterfall and a small trod. This can be followed down and around to the outflow of the lochan at NN 218 672. Cicerone's Joe Williams favours this route, but take care not to mistake it for the NE ridge, which is a much more scrambly option and not listed here!

When ascending Munro number 9 – Binnein Beag (Small Peak), runners might chose to make a beeline between the two small lochans and head for the loose red scree run on the west flank, but for most it's far simpler to use to the path up and down the south ridge. Follow a clear trod, with occasional handholds near the top. Out and back for walkers takes approximately 45 minutes. Bags can be left at the foot of the hill.

From the east shore of the largest lochan, take a stalker's path SE and then, turning a corner, go south into Coire a' Bhinnean. The path contours above the lower glen and into the head of the corrie. Walkers should follow the path for what feels like a little too long – starting to turn west – before crossing the burn and heading uphill on switchbacks. The path is a little vague at first but soon becomes clear, before topping out on a beautiful plateau jeweled with lochans and islands.

Runners might choose to shortcut these switchbacks and head straight for the foot of the next hill from around NN 221 661.

The path to Munro 10 – Sgùrr Èilde Mòr (Big Peak of the Hind) leads up the foot of its ridge, WSW, at approximately NN 225 657. It zigzags up through red dirt and screes, slightly left of the ridge. It is mostly loose and becomes very steep near the top of the crest. Upon topping out, turn left and continue up for a short distance to reach the summit cairn.

The 'valley section' from Sgùrr Èilde Mòr

After the tedium of that last ascent, the way off Sgùrr Èilde Mòr by its broad NE ridge is a balm for aching knees. It's a fast 2km of moss with only occasional quartz underfoot to slow progress. Where it begins to level out, you'll meet a stalker's path coming in from the left. Pass the first crag (680m) on your right and then veer left to join the second.

From here go down on awkward tussocks and heather. As you begin the descent aim off right of the summit of Meall a' Bhùirich on the other side of the glen. It's a free for all here, with no path at all, but this line is easier. At the foot of the slope there's a bog waiting – we are near the watershed here – so poles may come in handy. The glen is a wonderful place in good weather, but can be mean in bad weather and a midge and cleg-infested hell in high summer.

Meet the **Abhainn Rath** where it braids and ford the shallows. If in spate this may prove difficult. Now turn east to follow an intermittent path which runs alongside the river. It's best to stick fairly close to the water, crossing peat hags and occasional burns feeding in to the main water-course, heading towards **Meanach Bothy**.

Meanach can be a useful stopping point for backpackers, and has two rooms, both dry.

On the south side of the river, at NN 263 683, a small copse of trees surrounds the **Ruins of Luibeilt**. If you're coming from a support point at the head of Sgùrr Èilde Mòr, this is the place to cross the river. At times of high rain or thaw the Abhainn Rath can be in spate and impassable, so good information beforehand and team support if you're making a 24-hour attempt is useful here.

Joe Williams enjoys a brief pause on his clockwise round

NOTE FOR THOSE GOING CLOCKWISE

If meeting a support team at the ruin at the head of Loch Èilde Mòr, it's perfectly possible to ascend NW (or descend SE) on the flank of Sgùrr Èilde Mòr (see map – labelled 'often used ascent if travelling clockwise'). In ascent, head for the broad ridge to the south, over fairly easy heather and grass. The heather lessens and the ground becomes rockier at around 800m. Join a vague trod slightly to the left of the ridge at approximately NN 232 656 and continue over rougher, more bouldery ground for the final 200m to the summit cairn.

This is often the third leg for runners attempting the sub 24-hour Round, and for good reason. Na Gruagaichean is much easier in reverse, the rubbishy chute of Am Bodach is easier to climb than descend, and the ground between Stob Ban and Mullach na Coirean is fairly level and easygoing for those at the end of a very long run.

LEG 2

Luibeilt to Fersit – the valley section

Distance	14.6 miles (23.5km)
Ascent	4891ft (1490m)

This is a long section of glen, followed by stony track, before some rounded but very remote hills at the far end of the round.

The area around Luibeilt is the only sustained section of glen on the route, and given the remoteness of the Ramsay Round, it's a good place to consider options. If you do need to bail, it's possible to do so by heading west back down Glen Nevis, SSW to Loch Èilde Mòr and Kinlochleven, or NNW to the Lairig Leacach and Spean Bridge.

Assuming all is well at **Luibeilt**, cross the river with care if you need to and either head for **Meanach Bothy**, or stay riverside for slightly less tussocky going. The path towards **Loch Treig** starts boggy but soon dries out as you move east, following the river and descending past picturesque birch and rowan trees to a plain where cattle often graze.

Staoineag Bothy is your second option for a shelter in the area, and my personal preference. Solid, dry and mouse free, with two rooms downstairs and a large sleeping area upstairs. However, it does mean wading back across the river using the often submerged stepping stones, which depending on the conditions may not be possible. Plan accordingly!

From Staoineag, the path on the north side of the river climbs high over a shoulder and becomes very boggy before dropping to Creaguaineach. For those using the bothy, it's best to continue south of the river for a beautiful winding path through old woodlands to arrive at the bridge.

The start of the valley section at low water

Leaving Staoineag bothy, the best stretch of path on the valley section

Memories of Glen Nevis

In Staoineag Bothy, there's a sheet of remembrances hung on the wall – you might still see it. Angus Montgomery of Kirkintilloch remembers staying with his grandfather and family, a man called John Matheson, who was the stalker there until his death in 1922. His grandmother also died there. They were evacuated from nearby Chiarrain after the blackwater reservoir was built. They would arrange to meet with the nearest family, the Eliots of Luibeilt, for a Ceilidh about halfway between the two settlements. That place is now a reed bed, but this lonely glen was once inhabited and rang with music.

The flat ground around the ruined lodge of **Creaguaineach** makes a popular camping spot for backpackers and fishermen. Cross the bridge and continue east on well-maintained estate track to Lochtreighead. Follow the track around the loch and cross another bridge over the Allt a' Chamabhreac, which now has a run-of-river hydro scheme on it. This stretch can feel long and a little soulless.

A few hundred yards after the bridge at NN 341 680, cut east on open ground to meet the broad ridge of the next Munro, number 11 – Beinn na Lap (Dappled Hill). The ground can be wet low down, but it can be useful to use the upstream burn as a handrail for a while if visibility is really bad. Beinn na Lap has several false summits on the ascent. There's a faint argocat track a good way to the top, and the summit itself marked by a small shelter cairn. There are superb views across **Loch Ossian** and Rannoch Moor.

Head NNE for around 1km, following this rough, rocky ridge, and once you've descended slightly leaving the last of the crags on your right, bear north and descend very steeply off the hill. It's an awkward descent to the glen: streamlets, loose rock, grass and heather. At this stage aim directly for the wild and impressive corrie between Meall Garbh and Chno Dearg. Ford the Allt Feith Ealaidh (on OS maps, the Allt Feith Thuill), at this point just a burn, and then begin the equally tortuous ascent uphill, handrailing the burn that pours out of the corrie. From here, climb up the back of the corrie, or onto the ridge at the right (as shown on the map). It's not technical but it is steep.

Once on the plateau, aim slightly northwest for the bulk of Munro 12 – Chno Dearg (Red Nut or Red Hill). Navigation can be tricky here – the hills on the Treig side have more of a Cairngorm feel and are less obviously pointy than the Mamores.

After the summit cairn of Chno Dearg, descend southwest to the *bealach* and follow the undulating, stony ridge to the summit of Munro number 13 – Stob Coire Sgriodain (Peak of the Scree Corrie) There are two or three spot heights to get over before the summit itself, all offering incredible views of the whole round...which at this point is pretty much as far as the eye can see, west!

When descending Stob Coire Sgriodain, the descent path is straightforward at first and follows the ridge straight north. Runners have traditionally headed left off the hill at around 849m, aiming for the edge of the woodland in order to meet their checkpoint at the dam. It should be borne in mind that part of this route is very dangerous, and not suitable for those with backpacks.

For those not on the clock, the ground to the right offers a multitude of escape options to the beautiful (if long and damp) path that runs on the left-hand side of the Allt Chaorach Beag, aka the Fersit burn. There are some nice places to camp alongside but please avoid being in sight of the farm, as relationships between runners and the landowner have been delicate in the past. If you do decide to follow the nose of the ridge north

there are three or four small crags to be negotiated – downclimbing with a backpacking rucksack may be awkward for some. Follow the burn down to the bridge at **Fersit** farm and turn left for the settlement and round to the car park. From here take the Rio Tinto Alcan track south to the head of the dam.

NOTE FOR THOSE GOING CLOCKWISE

Leg 2 is, for both runners and walkers, often considered to be the toughest section. It's certainly the most 'out there' feeling. Of particular note for those travelling clockwise is the ascent of Beinn na Lap from the wild glen between it and Chno Dearg. If weather is bad or navigation challenged, follow the outflow from the hanging coire to the south of Chno Dearg, cross the burn and then head due south for Sron na Cloiche Sgoilte, thereby avoiding the screes on the upper section of Beinn na Lap.

For those tempted to stay south of the Abhainn Rath in order to meet a support team at Loch Èilde Mòr, the ground west of Staoineag Bothy can be incredibly boggy and slow going.

Snowy springtime conditions on Stob Coire Sgriodain

The second Stob Ban (Grey Corries) from the path from the Lairig Leachach bothy

LEG 3

Fersit to Glen Nevis YHA

Distance	20.9miles (33.7km)
Ascent	12,378ft (3770m)

This is the longest and most technical section of the Round, with the most climbing. It starts with a long stony ridge followed by the crux of the route and then onto the highest ground in the UK. This leg includes an exceptionally fine ridge traverse on quartz.

The next two Munros are often grouped together as The Easains, affectionately referred to as 'This Yin an That Yin'. Continue out past the dam on the track and then turn right up the hill onto a rougher track, which leads towards a fenced sheep shearing area – go through this, keeping the burn on your left as you head uphill. Cross the burn and emerge onto more open ground to the left of 'Pillar'.

Ascend Meall Cian Dearg with care – the nose can hold snow late in the season and is very steep. A faint path leads up to the east side of the nose and then contours around to the front, before switchbacks lead up fairly simply through the crags. It's very eroded in places and under snow the path won't be visible. Once breached the views open out and the broad ridge can simply be followed up, with Loch Treig on your left and the **Grey Corries** on your right. Pass the spot height of 977m before reaching the broken summit slabs of Munro number 14 – **Stob a' Coire Mheadhoin** (Peak of the Middle Corrie).

Munro 15 – **Stob Coire Easain** (Peak of the Corrie of the Little Waterfalls) lies ahead, an imposing chunk of smashed quartz. Descend southwest, round the corrie and follow the steep, rough path to the top. This steepens in the final metres and can hold snow too, so care is advised.

The descent from Stob Coire Easain is less of a slog than might first appear. Head ever so slightly south of straight west following a rib of grass from the summit. This crosses a band of loose rock and then turns into a broad, grassy thoroughfare, making for swift and easy progress. There is a band of scree on your left, which is easily avoided and if the weather is on your side you should have Binnein Beag, from whence you came, directly in your line of sight. The descent steepens and crosses more loose rocks before joining the headwaters of the Allt Ruigh na Braoileig and becoming boggy underfoot. Stick to the left of the drainage area until it begins to take you too far south, then begin to cross the burn channels that feed into the glen. This is more awkward, heathery terrain, which will be slower going, but is not at all technical.

Meet the path and cross it, heading over easy ground to ford the river. In periods of heavy rain this can be in spate, but it goes down quickly and there are several fording points.

Having forded the river, cross more flattish ground to meet the track. The Harvey's map route stays a little north of a burn, which may be useful as a handrail. Go up over heathery, boggy and occasionally rocky ground. Cross the second track (which goes over to Luibeilt) and keep right of the burn. Looking up you'll see a sort of green

runway – head for this. It takes you up onto a flatter, plateau-like area. From here, head to the left of the mounds and go up on short turf and moss to meet the shoulder of Munro number 16 – **Stob Ban** (being the second White Peak on the route). Join the path from the bothy.

For those staying at the **Lairig Leacach Bothy** (one room, dry, no fireplace), there is a path (which is not marked on the OS but is on the Harvey's map) that runs up to Stob Ban on the south side of the Allt a' Chùil Choirean. Go south from the bothy and cross this burn, heading uphill on a track. Take a right turn on a clear path which then disappears after minute or two. Make for the crag with the small tree hanging on its left. This beautiful alpine style path cuts up the centre of the crag before heading up a broad shallow gully (boggy in places). From here it cuts around the right hand of the shoulder summit (and not over it, as per the map) and gains the shoulder of Stob Ban proper.

From here, a good path snakes its way up the east ridge, with a few switchbacks near the top.

The Lairig Leacach Bothy, with Sgurr Innse behind

The blocky arête after the summit of Caisteil

In common with the other Stob Ban on the route, there is a false summit on the way up. From the actual summit, walk straight past the cairn, west and then down steeply NW over very loose quartz talus. The path braids, the left one being easier for those with backpacks. Follow it down to the Coire Rath, a magical place to camp. There are lochans here for water to be boiled – fresh water needs collecting from one of the burns to the west.

The climb up Munro number 17 – Stob Choire Claurigh (Peak of the Brawling Corrie, referring to the roaring of stags) is simple enough but there's a lot of it. A good path begins on the north side of the largest lochan at Coire Rath, initially following a rib of rock upwards. The path winds up, sometimes disappearing for a few metres at a time, then arriving at a flattish area with a few small pools of water. Continue up, climbing over bands of scree and then loose, quartz talus again to reach the summit cairn as soon as you top out. You'll be rewarded with spectacular views of the whole Round.

You are now at the start of one of the best high-level traverses in the UK, perhaps Europe – **The Grey Corries**, the Aonachs and Ben Nevis, collectively known as the Lochaber Traverse. This should present few problems after this much practice, and navigation is straightforward on a thin ridge. However, it can still take a good while to traverse over uneven rocky ground. The northern corries also hold snow late in the season, so watch out for rotten snow patches.

From the summit of Stob Choire Claurigh, go downhill WSW over quartz, following a clear path in between the bands of rock and stretches of grass on the lower ground. The path rises slightly to contour under Stob a' Choire Leith, before curving south to the impressive, craggy **Stob Coire Cath na Sine**. From here, head west to the summit of **Caisteil**, which entails a little descent before a climb. Just after this top is an exciting miniature arête littered with massive quartz blocks. Cross this narrow section and climb through bands of rock to reach a flat grassy area and the final approach to Munro 18 – Stob Coire an Laoigh (Peak of the Corrie of the Calf).

Descend WNW from the summit cairn for the bealach leading to Stob Coire Easain, which offers great views but is not officially on the round and is tricky to downclimb at its western end. Our route means going down into Coire Easain, but don't be tempted to head down too soon. Wait for the scree runs just before the start of the climb to **Stob Coire Easain** itself – there's a small 'nick' in the skyline. It's loose here but the rock is smaller and easier underfoot than the huge blocks beforehand.

Coire Easain makes an excellent campsite, with one or two small springs and flat, mossy ground. From the corrie, head up easy ground between glacial boulders and reach the bealach before Munro number 19 – Sgùrr Chòinnich Mòr (Big Peak of the Moss). Walk over granite terraces to reach the foot of the hill, which is simply climbed on a clear but sometimes steep and scrambly path up the NE ridge. The path follows a weakness on the eastern flank, mostly up grassy slopes and through the occasional rocky outcrop for the final, level ridge to the summit. It's a wonderful hill.

From the cairn, come off the hill SW on grassy slopes to a bealach and follow the path straight up its smaller sister – **Sgùrr Chòinnich Beag**. There's a path that splits off to the right and appears to traverse around the hill – don't be tempted, it really is easier to go over! Runners can skirt the grassy flat top on the south flank of the hill, and then make a descending traverse for speed's sake. Go down even more steeply to a broad bealach, suitable for camping but very dry, marked with a spot height of 731m.

There's a number of options for the climb onto Stob Coire Bhealaich, with a lot of height to be gained however you proceed. This is the crux of the round and is best attempted in good visibility (at least the first time you try it!)

Runners may choose to follow the terraces on the right-hand side of a large boulder field to the very steep ground above, known as 'Spinks' Ridge' (after Nicky Spinks, the former women's record holder for the Round – marked pink on the following page). This is absolutely not recommended for those with a backpack, as the higher

ground has become increasingly eroded over the last few years. In the summer months, runners also commonly use 'Charlie's gully' (topping out at approximately NN 206 706, marked blue) but be aware that this can hold snow and be impassable until late in the season.

There is a longer but easier route that takes a wide line up a grassy gully (marked green on the topo) but to my mind, the best route overall is as follows: First locate a green strip of fertile, mossy ground below a notch in the ridge above you – this is Charlie's Gully, which runs to the left of a burn. Then, locate the first low point on the ridge to the left of this gully. This is your final approach. With those as your guide, follow the path from the bealach uphill to find a dry-stone wall with steep crags immediately above. Turn left (SW) at the wall and walk on past the end of the crags, contouring diagonally uphill to cross a burn. Continue uphill to cross the lower part of Charlie's Gully, then head south around the corner of a headwall on vague deer trods. Using the headwall and another smaller burn as a handrail, head up steeply on terraces and over mud, grass and bands of scree, topping out north of **Sgùrr a' Bhuic** at approximately NN 205 704. See the topo, and the route marked in yellow.

From the ridgeline here, go west for a few yards before heading north uphill, circuiting around the worst of the boulder field. There's a path that hugs the ridgeline and goes past Charlie's gully before turning NW around to the summit of Stob Coire Bhealaich. Note that the path contours under the north ridge for a while. Clamber up through easy bands of rock to the summit, joining the ridge for spectacular views towards a dogleg north. The path splits here – take the right fork north, following the edge for the steady climb to the barren plateau of Munro 20 – Aonach Beag (Little Ridged Mountain) – with its tiny cairn.

From here, go NNW to find a good path down to the bealach before joining a very broad track that stays east of the middle of the broad ridge ahead and takes you up onto Munro 21 – Aonach Mòr (Big Ridged Mountain) – after 1 km. Follow the track to reach a huge cairn surrounded by very eroded ground.

The crux: Spinks' ridge is marked pink. Charlie's Gully is marked blue. The suggested route is marked yellow. A further route (green) takes a grassy rake and is easier, but longer.

The Grey Corries, with the Aonachs and Nevis in the distance, from Stob Choire Claurigh

To escape the Aonachs, make your return south, down the slope you just came up, but this time using another smaller path, which stays west of the main ridge. Locate a cairn at approximately NN 189 721, which indicates the start of a path down. In the past, runners (and guidebook writers!) have chosen to use the gullies to the north of this to exit the plateau but this is extremely eroded and growing more precarious on a yearly basis. I very much doubt the path is much, if at all slower, and it's definitely more environmentally-friendly. It hugs the north side of a westerly spur leading to the Bealach Coire Giubhsachan. After a little while, a burn emerges from the hillside on your right, which you cross lower down. It's steep and loose but far preferable to the gullies mentioned above. This path exits the slope directly opposite a stone wall, which is the marker for the climb onto Càrn Mòr Dearg.

The Bealach Coire Giubhsachan is an excellent camping spot with readily available water just over the *bealach* to the north.

From the *bealach*, take the trod immediately to the right of the stone wall. This first cuts left above the wall and then winds up through the crags before settling on the north side of the ridge. There are a couple of bulkheads to go up and over before the ridge thins, with the path just to the south of the crest. Head due west and up to meet the summit cairn of Munro number 22 – Càrn Mòr Dearg (Big Red Hill).

From here, go south down onto a thinning ridge which curves around the head of Coire Leis to meet Ben Nevis – also known as the Càrn Mòr Dearg (CMD) arête. The arête has a reputation, but this is possibly more a fact of the exposure and commitment needed, rather than technical difficulty. The path is clear at first but soon gives way to large boulders and blocks. If you are carrying poles it can be useful to stow at least one of them. For most of the trickier or more exposed sections there are escape paths – when heading due south on the first leg, these tend to be on the west side, and on the south side as the ridge bends west. On the second section a good deal of the climb can be bypassed under the crags to the south, before an easy scramble up to the *bealach* cairn at approximately NN 711 171.

NOTES FOR THOSE GOING CLOCKWISE

- The last leg for walkers is often the first leg for runners. As explained at the head of this section, this gets all the big climbs out of the way at the start of a timed round.

- Descending off Ben Nevis for CMD, it can be a good idea to use the metal navigation poles as a guide, so as not to overshoot the col.

- The route onto the west side of the Aonachs is much easier taken as a climb.

- Spinks' Ridge in descent; I'd urge even runners to consider the environmental benefits of resting this route for a few years to allow the turf to grow back and the route to consolidate again – it was in terrible condition at the time of writing.

The final climb of the Round is only 200m but is taxing, over large boulders. It can be helpful to follow the curve of the corrie around for a while to avoid some bands of rock to the southwest. After a few minutes, bear NW slightly to see navigation markers to the summit. Paths come and go either side of these metal poles, dependent on the size of the boulders. The boulders turn to smaller stones as the ground flattens out near the summit, where you will often be met by the surreal sight and sound of day trippers on the UK's highest mountain – Munro number 23 – Ben Nevis (Venomous Mountain, or possibly Mountain with its Head in the Clouds, or Mountain of Heaven).

It's not over yet. The main path down off the Ben is (obviously) the biggest descent of the round and a task in itself. The top is covered with deep snow for much of the year. From the summit cairn, follow the path if visible or three navigation cairns if not, on a grid bearing of 231 degrees for 150m. Then, handrail a longer line of navigation cairns on a grid bearing of 282 degrees. Continue in a straight line, following the cairns down from NN 161 712 to NN 157 713. There is a steeper section (called McLean's steep), after which the angle eases. Be aware of very steep and treacherous gullies on all sides, especially the old path zigzagging SW from the summit leading to Five Finger Gully, and use pacing and timing especially if visibility is compromised. From NN 157 713, the path switches back down in WNW direction.

Runners might choose to avoid the switchbacks and go down in a direct line on grass and scree, meeting each corner of the path in turn, but there is no need for walkers and backpackers to do this – please keep erosion to a minimum. There is a section called 'the grassy bank', banned on the Ben Nevis Race and which should be avoided altogether. The John Muir Trust (stewards of the summit) tell me that runners sometimes use another shortcut from NN 142 719, which contours round and joins the path at the corner, at NN 143 721. They also ask for all runners to be aware of their footfall, as this new shortcut may be more robust than the grassy bank, but cannot sustain too much use.

All users should use the main path past the halfway lochan. This section was very badly eroded from heavy footfall, but recent work done by the Nevis Landscape Partnership has improved the situation markedly. As you near the bottom, the path crosses a footbridge and meets birchwood, before the path splits. Take the left fork (signposted YHA) and return to the starting point by crossing the bridge over the river at the bottom.

Congratulations!

Practicalities

Getting there and around

By road, Fort William is reached via the A82 from Glasgow, or the A9 and the A86 (the Laggan road) from Edinburgh.

Public transport is also fairly direct: you can take a train from Glasgow Queen Street or from Edinburgh Waverley. The London train runs from Euston, and it's also possible (although expensive) to catch the sleeper train. There is also a good bus service (Scottish Citylink) from Glasgow to Fort William.

Once at Fort William (big supermarket and an outdoor store next to the station), take the Belford Road due east heading out of town, before turning off at the Ben Nevis Highland centre roundabout on the C1162. This runs alongside the River Nevis into the glen itself. You'll find the youth hostel and camping on the road. The walk should take 45 minutes to 1 hour.

Water

Water is cleaner and less scarce in Scotland as a rule, but the following is an incomplete list of places where burn or lochan water may be found to refill your bottle. Be aware that this is wild water and so please use your discretion to decide whether it needs treating or not.

1: The Mamores

- Lochan Coire nam Miseach.
- The col between Stob Choire a' Chàirn and An Gearanach – running water can be collected from the spring about 40m below the col to the SE, at NN 188 661.
- The lochan under Binnein Beag.
- Lochans to the east of Sgùrr Èilde Mòr. All these have water nearby.

Walkers high above Lochan Coire nam Miseach, leg 1

2: The Loch Treig and Easian Hills
- Allt Feith na h Ealaidh, between Beinn na Lap and Chno Dearg.
- Allt Chaorach Beag, the burn fed by Lochan Coire an Lochain, east of Stob Coire Sgriodain.

3: The Grey Corries and Aonachs
- Coire Ràth, north of Stob Ban. Pools for water to be boiled, running water can be collected by dropping north of the *bealach*.
- Coire Easain, between Stob Coire Easain and Sgùrr Chòinnich Mòr.
- *Bealach* at head of Coire Giubhsachan, between the Aonachs and Càrn Mòr Dearg.

Suggested backpacker's itinerary
The beauty of wild camping is that it can happen anywhere, and I am wary of supplying times, because everyone's pace is different. Overly specific information can lead some to make dangerous assumptions in the mountains. However, here is a loose guide that may be useful.

Day 1: The Mamores
Glen Nevis to a wild camp, either at the col under An Gearanach or at the lochan under Binnein Beag.

Day 2: The Glen
A shorter day, from An Gearanach or Binnein Beag, to Staoineag Bothy or Loch Treig.

Day 3: Loch Treig Munros
Staoineag or Loch Treig, to a wild camp by the Allt Chaorach Beag, above Fersit.

Day 4: The Easians
From Fersit to the Lairig Leacach Bothy.

Day 5: Grey Corries and the Aonachs
From the Lairig Leacach Bothy to a wild camp at the *bealach* above Coire Giubhsachan.

Day 6: CMD and the Ben
A shorter half day to finish over the final two obstacles.

Alternative ways to complete the Charlie Ramsay Round
Charlie Ramsay's open and inclusive perspective on his own Round was one of the chief inspirations behind this book. For Charlie, a Ramsay Round doesn't have to be done in a single push or within a certain timeframe. It's open to 'section-hikers' as well as 'through-hikers' and of course, runners – whether they are attempting the 24-hour challenge or not. There are a multitude of options for breaking the Round into sections, but here are a few ideas to begin with.

The Mamores
A long single day or easier two-day through route can be devised from Kinlochleven to Fort William (or vice versa), using bus 44 that runs between the two towns. There's good camping at Lochan Coire nam Miseach, the col between Stob Choire a' Chàirn and An Gearanach, the lochan under Binnein Beag or the larger lochans to the east of Sgùrr Èilde Mòr.

There are shorter options, too – Stob Ban and Mullach nan Coirean is a wonderful half-day trip with plenty of drama and some lovely forest trails that can be explored around the 'lower falls' car park.

The two spurs of the Mamores – Sgùrr a' Mhàim and An Gearanach – can be completed as part of a big, four Munro day, along with Stob Coire a' Chàirn and Am Bodach, known collectively as the Ring of Steall, a round which is even more exciting in winter conditions.

Finally, the eastern end of the range is very accessible on day walks from Kinlochleven. There are good bothies in upper Glen Nevis at the eastern end too – Meanach and Staoineag – which can help you join up subsequent stages, especially if the weather proves challenging.

The Loch Treig Munros
An excellent two-day variation of the Loch Treig Munros can be achieved starting and ending in Fersit, by descending south instead of west off Stob Coire Easain and heading towards Creagan a' Chaise. The ridge is interesting but entirely non-technical – rocky slabs higher up and historical subsidence lower down. At the bottom,

join a vague track alongside the Allt na Lairige SE to meet the waterfall and gorge near its exit into Loch Treig. It's possible to cross the river in the shallows as it meanders down if you wish; if not there's a bridge. Head towards the ruined Creaguaineach Lodge, then cross the bridge to regain the Ramsay Round route.

Charlie and his wife, Mary, have enjoyed this variant themselves, but starting and finishing at Corrour station instead of Fersit. Trains can be caught from Fort William to Corrour, daily. If you wish, a stay at Loch Ossian Youth Hostel means it's easy to further split this stage, doing Beinn na Lap and perhaps Chno Dearg and Stob Coire Sgriodain from there, and the two Easain Munros, west of Loch Treig, from the Fersit side.

It's also viable to use the Lairig Leacach Bothy as a stopover to access these Easians (Stob a'

Choire Mheadhion and Stob Coire Easian), perhaps taking in the two wonderful nearby Corbetts – Cruach Innse and Sgurr Innse – as well.

The Grey Corries and the Aonachs

From the drove road beginning at Corriechoille farm (parking space at NN 256 788), the circuit of Stob Ban and Stob Choire Claurigh is a wonderful day walk around some beautiful corries, perhaps returning to the Lairig Leacach Bothy, or heading back along the north ridge, taking in the 'subsidiary' Munro top of Stob Coire Gaibhre west of the Lairig. You also ascend by way of that same hill and extend the circuit west to include Stob Coire Easain and Sgùrr Chòinnich Mòr, returning to the car by way of the northerly spur of Beinn na Socaich and a forest ride.

Southwest across Loch Linnhe, from Mullach nan Coirean

Sgùrr Chòinnich Mòr and its sister peak Sgùrr Chòinnich Beag are also accessible from Glen Nevis as a day walk, as are both Aonach Mor and Aonach Beag. Park at the Steall Fall car park and walk what WH Murray called 'the best half mile in Scotland' up the gorge to Steall Meadows. From here, walk around the dogleg and turn east into the glen itself. Without snow on the ground, this is a far more pleasant way to access these hills in isolation than by the Nevis Range ski centre. Doing all four of these tops in a single day from the car would be fairly strenuous and best saved for the longer daylight hours of spring and summer. Alternatively, split it into two trips, or camp or bivi on the way.

The Nevis stage

An exhilarating hill day and a rite of passage in itself in winter, is the Ben by way of the CMD arête, which gives you the final two tops – Càrn Mòr Dearg and Ben Nevis itself. This is best accessed from the beautiful birch woods east of Fort William. A walk from the car park above Torlundy makes a charming alpine start. This can of course be reversed, starting up the tourist route to the Ben and coming down by the arête. There's also a magnificent journey into Coire Leis, and around right under the north face of the Ben to the halfway lochan, a magical day trip if the tops are in cloud.

The Lochaber Traverse

This is the name given to the longer stage joining the Grey Corries, the Aonachs and the Ben, with Spean Bridge at one end and Fort William at the other. There's a bus service (line 512) and a train between the two. For walkers, it's a lot to accomplish in a single day, so an overnight camp en route is encouraged should you not wish to rush.

The Tranter Round
The Tranter is the shorter Round upon which the Ramsay Round was based. Its 18 Munros, 58km distance and 6280m of ascent make it a very significant undertaking. It includes the Mamores, the Grey Corries, the Aonachs and Ben Nevis, but omits the five Loch Treig Munros that Charlie Ramsay added to create his own Round. For walkers, it's a 2–4 day outing, and like the Ramsay Round, it starts and finishes at the Glen Nevis Youth Hostel.

Places to stay
Here are a few campsite, youth hostel and bothy locations that may be useful if you are planning to 'section' the Round or if you need to accommodate support teams before or after a changeover. Please don't use bothies as changeover points; this can lead to conflict for the Round.
▪ Glen Nevis Youth Hostel. Web: www.hostellingscotland.org.uk/hostels/glen-nevis; tel: +44 (0) 1397 702336; email: glen.nevis@syha.org.uk.
▪ Glen Nevis campsite. Web: www.glen-nevis.co.uk/campsite; tel: 01397 702 191; email: holidays@glen-nevis.co.uk.
   Both are superbly situated at the start/finish of the route, with good facilities.

Stage 1: Upper Glen Nevis
▪ Meanach Bothy (NN 266 684).
▪ Staoineag Bothy (NN 295 677).

Stage 2: Loch Treig Munros
▪ Loch Ossian Youth Hostel; Web: www.syha.org.uk/where-to-stay/highlands/loch-ossian.aspx; tel: +44 (0) 1397 732207; email: lochossian@syha.org.uk.

Stage 3: Easains
▪ Lairig Leacach Bothy (NN 282 736), or numerous places to camp in the glen itself.

Support for runners
There are multiple options for support teams on the Round, but the following are often used, and are offered here as suggestions. Of those listed, the head of Loch Èilde Mòr, and Fersit are the most commonly used by runners. Please note that bothies should not be used as changeover points, as it may disturb other users.

1. Luibeilt, or the ruin at the head of Loch Èilde Mòr
Regardless of whether the runner prefers to follow the ridge to the Abhainn Rath or descend to the head of Loch Èilde Mòr, a support team can go in via Kinlochleven. The lower gate to the Mamore Lodge is now regularly locked without warning, so it's wise not to leave support vehicles on that road in case they are locked in.
   You should either:

▪ Park at the Grey Mares Tail car park (free) and walk in, following signs for Loch Èilde Mòr (take the right-hand fork in the woods, a few minutes from the car park). This takes approximately 2½ hours.

▪ Or, leave vehicles at the foot of the Lodge road and walk or cycle in. This will take approximately 1–1½ hours cycling, or 2½ hours on foot. This road is being resurfaced to allow new hydro works.

2. Lochtreighead
A support team can be placed at the old lodge at Creaguaineach, with a team coming in from Corrour station, which is a walk of approximately 1 hour.

3. Fersit
The only road support on the Ramsay. Park vehicles at the car park and walk the short distance (10 minutes) to the dam to wait for runners using the traditional route. Note that no vehicles are permitted at the dam. Walkers will come via the public car park. Signage suggests that no overnight stays are permitted. Although this is not legally enforceable, please be considerate of local wishes. Fersit is a potential hotspot for the Ramsay Round and the landowner has to manage access to both the dam and the railway over his land, as well as the public.

4. Lairig Leacach

Support can come in from Spean Bridge in the north, via Corriechoille Farm. It's possible to drive vehicles on a rough track as far as a parking space at NN 256 788, just before the gate to the Killiechonate Woods. From there it's a walk of approximately 1½ hours. It's tricky (though not impossible) to cycle with loaded bikes, because the main gates on the south side of the woods have sometimes been padlocked (illegally), in which case bikes have to be passed over the top.

There should be an agreed place on the track west of the Allt na Lairige where the runner is due to come down from Stob Coire Easain and cross the river, in order that the support team can be there to meet them. Lairig Leacach Bothy is just north of the usual runner's route, and could be used to house supporters before or after a changeover but should not be used for the changeover itself.

5. Aonach Mor

A team could come in using the Nevis Range ski centre gondola and meet runners on the plateau. Please check times and availability before you travel (www.nevisrange.co.uk/mountain-gondola/ or +44 (0)1397 705 825).

Rules for runners

Runners attempting the sub 24-hour challenge must:

- Start and finish at Glen Nevis Youth Hostel.
- Climb all of the Munros in consecutive order, travelling either clockwise or anticlockwise.

You are permitted to contour around some of the minor tops if you wish, but you must visit all the Munros in the correct order.

Charlie recommends using pacers and support teams from a safety point of view on a timed attempt. He no longer records whether a Ramsay Round has been completed solo or unsupported.

Should you not want to engage support teams at the end of each leg, food drops are technically permitted although, as he points out, 'some purists would have difficulty in defining this option as being unsupported'.

Charlie is the keeper of the Round records and asks that you get in touch ahead of your Round attempt, as well as afterwards to let him know the details. This should include your full name, finish date, finish time, whether you did the route clockwise or anticlockwise, and a brief written report including your schedule. His email is charlieramsay15@gmail.com. He takes an active interest in timed attempts and may even come along to show support. Please note that Jon Broxap no longer keeps the records for the Fell Runners' Association.

Regarding winter attempts, Charlie uses the Metrological Office definition of winter – 1 December to 28 February. There's more discussion about what constitutes a winter Round in People of the Rounds.

Charlie Ramsay gathers himself for the off on the 1978 attempt © Charlie Ramsay collection

The history of the Round

The story of the Scottish Round can't be told without reference to two others – the Bob Graham and the Tranter. You've read about the former, but what about the latter?

Charlie explains: 'Ramsay's Round is an extension of Philip Tranter's Round established in June 1964, when Philip and his friend Blyth Wright planned a journey that involved travelling anticlockwise from Glen Nevis and climbing the 18 Munros that surround the glen, including 10 across the Mamores, four over the Grey Corries, the two Munros – Aonach Beag and Aonach Mòr – and the final 2 Munros of Càrn Mòr Dearg and Ben Nevis, Great Britain's highest mountain. It's a distance of 36 miles (57km) with a height gain of 20,000ft (6069m).'

Philip Tranter was a civil engineer and the son of Nigel Tranter, the historical novelist, who in turn was based just down the road from Charlie, in Gullane on the Lothian coast. Working at Edinburgh's Commonwealth Pool in the early 1970s, Charlie had yet to hear of either of these

mountain challenges. He was content to use his lunch hour to get some air, running up and down nearby Arthur's Seat, and entering the odd 5 and 10-mile race. Charlie's boss – Louis – mentioned his exploits to the Scottish journalist and outdoorsman Tom Weir, who failed to be impressed and replied with a mention of the Ben Nevis Race.

In 1974, Charlie ran the Ben Nevis Race and finished in 1hr 50min, 38th overall. A year later he was invited to join Lochaber Athletic Club (AC). 'Everyone there was talking about Tranter's Walk, but it was impossible to find out anything about it.' From the office, Charlie called Tom Weir, and he filled in the details. 'He was a mine of information. Once again, I had to be thankful to Tom Weir. In a roundabout way, he had a part to play in the history of the Round.'

Charlie first did Tranter's Round in 1977: 'I'm not sure how many times I've done it, but it was always sub 24 hours – about 18 hours. I went both ways – clockwise and anticlockwise.'

Back in the city, he met up for lunchtime runs with a Kendal stonemason who was working on the building opposite the pool. In that year, Boyd Millen became the first person to run the double Bob Graham with a time of 52hr 30min.

Shortly after, Charlie met up with Boyd again while he and his family were on a summer camping holiday in the Lake District. Both men were flushed with success. Boyd asked Charlie to join him on Monday evening at 7pm for a jog up Skiddaw. Charlie continues: 'When I arrived, there was Chris Brasher, Paddy Buckley and George Rhodes, all trying for the Round.' There was another guy there – one of the original pacers for Bob Graham himself – Phil Davidson – plus a few other stalwarts, Joss Naylor for one. I had no idea what I was doing there!'

"When I arrived, there was Chris Brasher, Paddy Buckley and George Rhodes, all trying for the Round."

Charlie was now implicated in Brasher's first attempt (of three) at the Bob Graham Round, but he hadn't made his involvement official with the club beforehand: 'I wasn't officially a pacer at all; I was the mule carrying the gear for Chris, just pinned on.'

On the top of Skiddaw, he was asked to carry on to Blencathra. At Threlkeld the same question was repeated: Would he stay on until Dunmail Raise? Boyd agreed to get a lift back to the campsite and let Charlie's wife Mary know what was afoot. 'I didn't quite believe that he would, but when we arrived at Dunmail, Paddy retired, Joss left to go to London and meet Muhammad Ali for lunch, and Boyd came on as a pacer. But he'd also brought my tracksuit, which was proof that he'd

Charlie Ramsay and pacers at Glen Nevis. © Charlie Ramsay collection

been to see my wife, and the green light for me to continue.'

Had he run this before? 'No! I didn't know the route at all, but I was with people who knew the route very well.'

At Wasdale, Chris was very sick. His regular *Observer* column of the time ('Breath of Air') tells that he made it as far as the summit of Yewbarrow, before heading to Joss Naylor's farm for a glass of milk from Joss' wife, thereby ending his attempt.

Brasher continues: 'And Charlie? He gave up pacing at Wasdale and became a contender, taking off at great speed with our fittest pacer, Chris Brad, going through hell in the noonday sun on Red Pike and Kirk Fell but finishing strongly through the lanes into Keswick.'

As Charlie remembers it, Fred Rogerson bent the rules a little at Wasdale: '"OK", he said, "you've come all this way, you can carry on".'

Charlie got round in 21hr 57min, becoming club member number 82. That evening, he was invited out to dinner by Chris and his team. 'I came off the hill at about 5pm, and we went out that evening. The whole family – Mary, Grant and Ashley – we all went. We thought it was great; we'd been eating beans and fish fingers and living in a tent all week. A full meal that included a starter, main course, desert and coffee was not on our holiday list! Chris asked me if there was an equivalent to the Bob Graham Round in Scotland, and if not, would I like to set one up? I felt like I had a sense of the model now. All I did was extend Tranter's Round, because I knew the area well by then. Over winter, I looked at the map and by adding in the five Treig Munros, I could see that it would bring it up to around the same mileage as the Bob Graham.'

Teams of pacers were assembled from the ranks of Charlie's club, Lochaber AC, and the date was set for Saturday 8 July 1978. Charlie offered to raise money for Lochaber Mountain Rescue and they used his attempt as a radio training exercise, as well as to ensure safety. He did reconnoitre

"The good thing about the Mamores is that you're knocking Munros off every 45 minutes or so, so psychologically that keeps you upbeat."

the full Round beforehand, 'which took about 30 hours – I had to have a little kip on the way'.

Charlie goes on to describe the challenge itself. 'On the day, I enjoyed the climbing – particularly the Mamores, because I was fit and fresh. The good thing about the Mamores is that you're knocking Munros off every 45 minutes or so, so psychologically that keeps you upbeat. I hated the valley section, but I got excited again at the end. I enjoy the boulder hopping, the more technical stuff.

'After the valley section, I got to the foot of Beinn Na Lap about 10pm. I'd already had enough, I couldn't find my footing in the dark. For the first part of the descent to Fersit Dam we couldn't see any head torches from our transition point. At that time, a support crew could drive down to the dam from the car park – access gates prevent that now. After a few hundred metres, we could see the torches and car headlights. It was a relief to see family and friends and get fed, watered, fresh clothes and kit, and a fresh pacing partner.

'On the Grey Corries, the mist cleared and everything was lit up, it was phenomenal. We got to the Aonachs, and I dropped my running partner off – he was knackered. I got a little lost on the Aonachs before finding the gully that would lead me to Càrn Mòr Dearg. If you look at my schedule you'll see it took me over an hour to get to Aonach Mòr – I was all over the place!

'I got down to the *bealach* between the Aonachs and the CMD and I thought I'd blown it, then suddenly I realised I was at about 2500ft. – I didn't have 4000ft still to climb to get onto the Ben, only 2000ft. On the CMD arête, I went along the top. With hindsight, it was probably a bit silly to boulder hop on my own at that stage. On the top of the Ben were a few members of Lochaber Mountain Rescue. I was planning on doing a handstand at this point, but I only managed a brief wave before starting the descent.

'I used the line one would normally use on race day, missing out the zigzags, then straight down the grassy slope and down to the youth hostel.

Looking south to the Mamores from the head of Coire Guibhsachan

That line down the grassy slope is off limits these days because of erosion. It helped that the finish line was a lot nearer than the finish for the Ben Nevis Race at Claggan Park, plus I was on very familiar ground. By then, it was 'game on' – it felt like the Round was going to become a reality.

'I think the Philip Tranter round is phenomenal, and how I extended it makes it tougher. To be honest, the valley section is probably the boring and difficult bit, but taken as a whole, it adds to the quality of the challenge.'

Charlie's record time of 23hr 58min lasted for the next nine years. It's difficult to do a direct comparison because the rules for each of the Rounds are so different, but to give a sense of just how much of a challenge the Ramsay is, at the time of writing there were only 114 successful sub 24-hour attempts of the Ramsay, and only five of those come in under 20 hours. By comparison, on the Paddy those numbers are 122 and 8, and on Bob Graham it's 2170, with a figure currently 'between 90 and 100' for sub 20-hour attempts (Bob Whitman). One would expect the latter to have more successful finishers, because it has existed for much longer, but those figures also tell us something about relative difficulty.

Charlie continues: 'For the next few years, the Round wasn't well known at all, and I was busy raising a family. But in 1986, Chris was on a business trip to Edinburgh and called in. He asked me to talk him through what I'd done, and of course, Chris being Chris, he wrote and talked furiously about it, and it slowly became what it's become.'

The following year, Martin Stone was the first to beat Charlie's time with a new record of 23hr 24min. Once again, we see the lines of connection between the Big Rounds writ large, and it couldn't have gone to a better contender: Martin was one of the pacers on Billy Bland's 1982 Bob Graham Round, a record Billy held for 36 years until 2018.

A runner's story: Jasmin Paris

Jasmin is the current record holder for the Charlie Ramsay Round, and this is the account of her record-breaking run in 2016, in her own words.

A year ago, almost to the day, I had been descending at break-neck speed off Ben Nevis in the wake of Jon Ascroft as he was lowering the Ramsay Round record, set but one month earlier, by about one hour. On 18 June this year, I was descending Ben Nevis again with Jon at my side to improve his time by another 45 minutes, setting a new record (not 'ladies record', just 'record') of 16hr 13min 53sec.

I opted to run anticlockwise, finishing on Ben Nevis. The alternative, Ben Nevis first, seems to be a more popular option and is the direction Nicky Spinks ran when she set the previous female record. It has the advantage of saving the easier

running along the Mamores for the end. However, finishing with the descent of the Ben is, from the aesthetic perspective, clearly the way to go.

As with my Bob Graham Round, I was keen to keep the attempt quiet and make sure it was fun. I contacted a small group of friends with whom I enjoy running and trust with lines, asking if they would provide the necessary support. I was very lucky – and grateful to people giving up their own time – to be able to assemble full support teams for two weekends in early June. As always, my mum was to provide road support and the cakes, which by now seem to be becoming legendary among pacers.

The team for leg 1 gather before Jasmin's record-breaking run: (l-r) Tom Harris, Graham Nash, Mark Harris, Alena Vencovska (Jasmin's mum), Charlie Ramsay, Jasmin Paris, Jonathan Whilock

Jasmin Paris and the Grey Corries ahead

After postponing the first weekend due to bad weather, on Saturday at 3am, under the light of a full moon, we set off.

Inside the forest, the night was warm and still, and we were glad when we reached the open hillside, away from the midges. The first light of dawn appeared, and we turned our head torches off as we neared the summit of Mullach nan Coirean. We arrived around three minutes up on Jon Ascoft's split, and I made a mental note of the pace, which seemed fairly comfortable, although my pacers, weighed down by copious quantities of my food, might say otherwise (I was struck by the way that supporters on this leg disappeared and reappeared at regular intervals, almost as if the support effort was being run as a relay). The sky turned pink, orange and purple, and we marvelled at the sight of the clouds of fog cascading in a waterfall over the 4000'ers and Grey Corries to our left.

The out-and-backs of Devil's Ridge and An Gearanach were fantastic, just the sort of scrambly stuff I love. As we arrived on Binnein Beag the cloud came in, shrouding us in white. Reassuringly for me, Graham led the descent of the North Ridge with no hesitation, and onwards on a direct line up the scree slope to Binnein Beag. At this stage, it was just the two of us, and since Graham was carrying my clothes/kit, rather than any of my food, he fed me from his own supplies. We then dropped down to the track, and rejoined the rest of the team for a companionable ascent of Sgùrr Èilde Mòr. From there we descended along the northeast ridge until it flattened out, and then headed diagonally across to the changeover point we'd agreed upon beforehand, 22 minutes ahead of Jon's schedule.

"However, finishing with the descent of the Ben is, from the aesthetic perspective, clearly the way to go."

Borne along by the enthusiasm of my fresh support team, we made good progress along the valley towards Loch Treig. Despite it not even being 9am, the day was growing hot, and I was glad we'd had such an early start. From that point onwards I lay down in every river I crossed, like a sheepdog in summer. We hit the track and started the steady climb up to the railway, and I allowed myself to walk a little before picking up the pace again. At the railway, we were met by the welcome sight of Charlie and Mary (Ramsay), and thus re-supplied with cake we started the climb of Beinn na Lap. At this point I was feeling a bit sick, but I put my head down, and trudged on up, until a quick side stop, which did much to improve the situation.

Nearing the summit of Chno Dearg, we met a lone runner coming in the opposite direction on his solo Ramsay Round. Having been prepared beforehand by Charlie that this would happen, we laughed, and shouted 'Hello Joe' (Williams, of Cicerone!) and 'Hello Jasmin' respectively, before embracing in a rather sweaty hug. Thus re-enthused, I sailed through the easy next section to the summit of Stob Coire Sgriodain, before dropping down the rough tussocky descent to the dam at Fersit, and the site of the second changeover.

In a scene rather reminiscent of the Wasdale changeover on my Bob Graham Round, the support team had only just arrived. Still, it did nothing to detract from the atmosphere, which was truly buzzing. I was at this point 49 minutes up on Jon's schedule, and was still running well. The record was looking distinctly achievable. That said, I had been with Jon on the last leg of his record round, and I knew how fast he'd been going – I was expecting to lose some of the buffer I'd accumulated. The question was how much, if any, I'd have left at the end...

I stayed only a couple of minutes, long enough to get sprayed down (rather like a horse) with suntan cream and to consume an unconventional combination of chocolate milk and roast potatoes, before setting off on the climb of Stob a' Choire Mheadhoin. Accompanied by locals Jon Gay and Finlay Wild, I was in excellent hands, and had no concerns about navigation whatsoever. I was aware that I was getting tired, but was still enjoying myself on what was really a very beautiful day. When we arrived at Lairig Leacach I lay down in it for almost a minute, whilst Finlay and Jon poured water on my head. Thus cooled, I was better able to face the climb of the second Stob Ban, although I can't have been feeling that great, since I asked for a gel (which I'd intended to do

only when things started to get hard, knowing what they have done to my digestive system on previous occasions).

We pushed on to Stob Choire Claurigh, where Jon Ascroft joined us. The ridge of the Grey Corries was splendid, with views spreading out all around us, and the distinct feeling of being homeward-bound. Climbing Spinks' Ridge up to Aonach Beag was hard work.

By the time we started the ascent of Càrn Mòr Dearg, I was beginning to feel I had done it. I'd lost a few minutes to Jon over the last few splits, but there was no way – unless I fell – that I could lose 45 minutes between now and the end. This knowledge, the company, and the scenes, worked together to carry me to the summit. We took the easy 'chicken run' route, along the left side of the Càrn Mòr Dearg arête, before the final ascent to Ben Nevis, for which I used my arms as much as I could to help my struggling legs.

Reaching that final summit plateau, and climbing the cairn, was both emotional and exhilarating, but I didn't hang around to enjoy it. Instead, we started the well-known helter-skelter descent, dodging tourists as we went. Finlay led the way, and I followed in Jon Ascroft's company, slithering and sliding down the scree and boulder sections, much as we had done one year earlier (on Jon's record Round), and two years earlier (on our shared Tranter).

I heard the sweet sound of bagpipes drifting up from the valley below. I was scarcely conscious of it at first, but as the sound of it started to sink in, so did the realisation of what I'd achieved. That final run-in along the bridge, getting sprayed with champagne, hugging Jon...it was all a bit surreal, and simultaneously wonderful. I staggered around for a bit on unsteady legs, we drank the bubbly, took some photos, and then headed to the pub to recount the day's adventures over burgers, beers and chips.

"By the time we started the ascent of Càrn Mòr Dearg, I was beginning to feel I had done it."

Jasmin Paris checks her watch minutes
before the off (on her record breaking
Charlie Ramsay Round)

People of the Rounds

ADVICE, INSIGHTS AND STRATEGIES FROM THE HILL RUNNING COMMUNITY

As we've seen, dig down into the history of the Rounds and the common thread is those that run them. Each of the three routes was brought into being by those who shared information, kept each other company on 'recces' (reconnoitres) and paced each other on attempts. It's an ethos that continues today, facilitated through online forums, regional running clubs and race meetings. There is plenty of banter and competitive spirit, and above all there is mutual support regardless of background. Mountain friendships can be among the most enduring, and in the story of the Rounds these friendships cut clean across both class and regional divides. In the case of how Ramsay's Round came to be, for example, Oxbridge journalists run and then dine with Edinburgh rec' officers and Kendal stonemasons.

It's a defining characteristic of both hill running in general and the Big Rounds in particular. Here are three big routes, in three very unique countries, but through a love of moving freely and unfettered in the open, we enjoy a shared culture. When we travel these trods, in very literal terms

we re-create that fellowship. Runners might start with one Round, perhaps the Bob Graham or maybe the one in their home country, and then make haste for the others – busy, gangly pilgrims meeting, sharing, pushing each other to do better. Mountain people travel, and travel broadens the mind. The simple act of putting one foot in front of the other brings people together.

The aim of this final chapter is to gather some of that expertise together and continue the sharing tradition. Friends and Round creators Paddy Buckley and Charlie Ramsay appear again, as does Wendy Dodds for her defining role in the Welsh Round. While it wasn't possible to speak to Bob Graham himself, Helene Whitaker, Nicky Spinks and Jasmin Paris are all hill running legends who have valuable advice across the three Rounds. Mike Hartley and Keri Wallace offer unique perspectives on their individual takes on the Big Three in one go, and Jim Mann generously shared his unparalleled winter experience. There are so many people it would have been great to speak to. Perhaps next time...

Llyn Edno (leg 1, Paddy Buckley Round)

Paddy Buckley

'Marvellous country'

Paddy came late to fell running at age 50, after a lengthy hill apprenticeship as a rock climber and long-distance walker. He started to run in a 'Thursday night club' and his first race was Pendle.

Paddy first met Charlie Ramsay through Chris Brasher. Both were pacers for Brasher's attempt on the Bob Graham (a story told in the section telling the history of the Charlie Ramsay Round). Subsequently, he and Charlie would meet for runs, both on Charlie's home turf on the Pentlands, and in Loanhead, where Paddy was living at the time while building a concrete boat he later attempted to sail to Patagonia! Later in life, he was part of the 'Fleetfoot' business, distributing New Balance running shoes for Chris Brasher.

Paddy tried the Bob Graham twice after the Chris Brasher attempt before succeeding. Originally, the Welsh Round was only intended as a way of practising for the Cumbrian one. He knew the Welsh Hills well. His wife Sally was Welsh and had quarrymen ancestors that had moved from the Lake District in 1798 to work in the Diffwys quarry in Ffestiniog.

He remembers Brasher's aversion to including Crib Goch as being down to the fact that 'he wasn't a very good rock climber!' Paddy's own time is 'around 26 hours'.

'I carried a small route card, with grid bearings and times written in pencil. I ate Butty Bananas, and water – soggy and easy to get down! Staminade worked for some people but not for me.

'I am old fashioned, but things change. People are so much fitter these days, they train more. Refinements, like doing the Rounds solo, or doing them in winter, will continue. People will always rise to the challenge.

Paddy Buckley at home in his library

'I'm delighted when people write to me to say that the Round helped them to make new discoveries – marvellous country, they say.'

Wendy Dodds, climbing hard on the Wasdale race

Wendy Dodds

'More a mountaineer than a runner'

Wendy is a retired physician and rheumatologist and a veteran hill runner. In 1982, she was the first person to complete the Paddy Buckley Round. She was the first woman to complete the 50 at 50 Lake District Challenge, and has run more Original Mountain Marathons than any other person. She ran in the first (and only) women's pair in the original Dragon's Back Race (with Sue Walsh, whose account of the Paddy Buckley Round features in A runner's story: Sue Walsh) and raced in the next as the eldest participant, aged 61.

What common issues are there for contenders?
'I have seen fit folk come to grief and seen much slower club members get round. On the 24-hour Rounds, it is probably more a psychological challenge...assuming that you have put in the training, gone over the route, and you have your food and fluid perfected.'

What experience is needed for the Rounds?
'I was a swimmer in my youth, then an orienteer. From there, I did Long Distance Walker's Association events before entering specific running events. I ran in road marathons as well as fell races – 15 marathons up to the age of 40. You need to consider that your pace is more variable off road, and there is a need to navigate. Providing you are fit, hill running is more in the head than the body.

'Personally, I think that we are seeing more inexperienced runners coming along to fell races to "give it a go". They may believe that because they have run the same distance or more on road and trails, they can do it on the hill too. But these are often hostile environments.'

What's distinctive about these three Rounds in your view?
'Remoteness, and navigation. If you need to stop, you can be a long way from help. The Bob Graham may be the most straightforward in that regard, but in bad weather you can get lost on any of the Rounds – even on the 'easy' sections, which are usually run during the night. Ultras are usually marked routes. The Big Three are not.'

Do you think being part of a club helps with preparation for the Rounds?
'I am proud to have been a member of Clayton-Le-Moors Harriers for more than 35 years. For challenges, there is always offer of support there. We have great fun in relays, and on long races there are usually lots of supporters. It is the camaraderie and peer support that act as encouragement to do more.'

Why do you run?
'It allows me to cover more ground in a given time than walking, and at times allows me to reach isolated places that would require a bivi if not running. I consider myself more a mountaineer than a runner.'

Charlie Ramsay

'The key thing is preparation'

Charlie Ramsay, a former time trials cyclist and swimming recreation officer for Edinburgh council, first began running up Arthur's Seat in his lunch hour, as a break from the chlorinated atmosphere of the Royal Commonwealth Pool. The full story of how his Ramsay's Round came to be is told in the previous chapter.

Are there common issues arising from reading the reports? Where do contenders get caught out?

'Folk run into trouble from a lack of Round familiarity. Another common problem is that people go out too fast. Going clockwise, they get to Fersit 10 minutes up on schedule, and pay the price on the valley section. That valley section is deceptive, because there's a slight gradient uphill and it's long. After the tops, it can feel really warm, too. People lose ground there because they want to get Nevis and the Aonachs out of the way, they go out like the clappers and haven't paced the whole Round properly.

'For those going clockwise, Loch Èilde Mòr is a difficult changeover. After a long valley section, the track to the loch is stony and rough underfoot. The climb from there is really long and intimidating – you've lost a lot of height and have to regain it all.

'The woods under Mullach nan Coirean can also be tricky. A clear forest route is still incomplete, although there are paths through the clearfell now, and the odd wee cairn to show the way.'

Can you talk about scheduling an attempt?

'I have a proposed schedule on my website, but that's just a starting point to build your own – what's good for me will not be good for you. Are you better at climbing or descending, how much night navigation have you done, at what point on the Round will you be feeling most tired? Then there's your team mates – how are your pacers at all those things, and who is at each changeover point? Some people prefer technical ground, others like flatter grassier terrain, some people like it warm, others hate the rain, and so on. Find out your strengths and weaknesses, on the ground – it really has to be based on you as an individual, and not on a desktop exercise.'

What about putting a pacing team together?

'First, they need to run at your pace, and be the kind of people that are happy to work for your attempt. You also want people you can endure for eight hours – they need to be matched in personality to you at different parts of the Round, not just there because they were available!

'This is another reason why you need to reconnoitre the whole thing. When I set out to do my attempt, I said "I'm going to reconnoitre all of it, so I know the way, and the pace I want to set at that point". If you don't do that prep, there's the risk of either being burnt off, or held back.

'The other thing I would say is – don't stretch your pacers. There are examples of attempts where pacers have been asked to do an extra leg because the team were short on a changeover, and it's nearly ended badly. Your support is there to support you, but it's your job to know their limits, or else they can become a liability.

'This whole area is a difficult one, and even more difficult when you are all waiting for a weather window. If you postpone by a day or two, can your team accommodate that delay? They might well have work, family and other responsibilities, so you can't be overly reliant on anyone for a particular section or skillset.

'What's driving all this is **you**, and everyone and everything else slots in behind you. The key thing is preparation. If you want success, then you must prepare – no compromise. And part of your preparation is gathering a team of people around you that you know and that know you.'

Charlie Ramsay, at home in Edinburgh

What's the role of a club?

'It helps build your network of people with the necessary skills and background. There may be a small contingent within a club that are keen or have suitable contacts, and sometimes there are folk there that are experts on each particular section of the Round. There are also those who are better suited for the other logistics – transition area duties, accommodation, and transport arrangements.'

Have you any advice about food and drink?

'My opening phrase is "I'm not a nutritionist!" You know your body better than I, you have your own pet foods, but I would say keep yourself fuelled up at all times, and if you are not sure, seek professional advice. If you do the training that's needed – 14 and 16-hour days, then you'll get a feel for what's needed for you personally.

'When I did it, we had jam sandwiches, tins of rice pudding, bacon rolls at Fersit, plenty of fruit – loads of bananas, and chocolate digestives and sweets. Smarties and raisins were a favourite, but I'd try and save them until near the end, for an extra (but short-term!) energy boost. We tried to get some sponsorship from Robinsons; they sent us juice, so we had lots of that. I had a young family; I couldn't very well eat steak while they ate cornflakes!'

The rules on solo and unsupported attempts differ between the Rounds. Can you talk about that?

'Solo and unsupported attempts are both things I find difficult to define and manage. My own take on this is that it would mean contenders are not committed to others, the weight of the food, clothing and kit needed for a successful attempt is increased, and their safety would be compromised. They should also leave details of their plan with friends, family and Police Scotland to facilitate being found in the event of the unforeseen.

'There have been cases where two contenders have completed the Round together, but still claim solo and unsupported. Or, do one section with support and another without. Others have assistance at changeover points or on the hill, or made use of a rucksack drop at strategic areas of the Round.

'Under these circumstances, I will always favour an attempt being supported, but if the contender wishes their challenge to be solo and unsupported, so be it. In 2014, I deleted the solo unsupported column from the Round records. I now only record their finishing number, name, finishing date, finishing time and direction of travel.'

What about winter Rounds? There's been a bit of controversy as to what qualifies...

'For the Ramsay, I use the UK Meteorological Office definition – 1 December to the end of February. Obviously, conditions can vary during that time, and are difficult to define. Is it snowing to the glen floor, is it fresh powder or icy up top? People use all sorts of subjective terms: great, Artic, challenging, severe, perfect, and classic... the list goes on.

'It is worth saying that a winter Round is still run in up to 16 hours of darkness, over two night sections. Otherwise I refrain from judgements and ask contenders to put the detail about conditions into their personal report.'

What got you started?

'I used to be a competitive cyclist with the White Heather Cycling Club in my youth, but when I went to London, I sold my bikes. I walked to work, then I started running there, or back, or both. When I returned to Edinburgh, a bike was not a priority for me, because of the hills where I lived and worked. I'd run first thing in the mornings in the Pentland Hills before work, and when possible I'd take a lunchtime run in Queens Park just to

get away from the swimming pool environment. I just enjoyed keeping fit.'

How important is competition?
'I ran the odd road race unattached to any club before my first Ben Nevis race in 1974. A year later, I joined Lochaber AC. Going up and down the hills, I thought it was great. There were not many runners doing that sort of thing in those days. But I wasn't that focused on the racing as a priority. My wife Mary will tell you that I was sometimes better at training than in the race. On the bike, I enjoyed time trials much more than road racing – at that

time, I was a shorter distance person, doing 10, 25, and 50 miles, and then you get older and your endurance improves. For me, that love of racing against the clock carried on into the hills.'

Nicky Spinks

'It's a big commitment, and the Rounds deserve that'

Nicky is a farmer and long-distance fell runner. Since she began running in 2001, she has set women's records for the each of the three Rounds described in this book, which she held until 2016. She currently holds the record for the double Bob Graham Round and is the only person to have run all three Rounds as doubles. She also holds the women's record for the Joss Naylor Lakeland Challenge, and the women's record for the number of Lakeland hills in 24 hours.

Nicky Spinks at home in her kitchen

Which is the hardest round?

'It's a toss-up between the Paddy and the Ramsay. The Paddy is more technical, rockier, and if the rocks are wet then it's harder. The Ramsay logistically is more difficult, and it's further north, so for southerners it's harder to reconnoitre. It's remote – you can't just go for a few hours, it takes that long to get there. They're probably equal in difficulty, but in different ways. It also depends what you like, whether you prefer rock or heather

bashing! If you don't like exposure, then the Ramsay is more challenging.'

Which is your favourite?

'It's probably ended up being the Paddy, because I spent more time on it than the others. I tried twice before I succeeded the third time. It was my initiation into getting faster, too. When I did the Bob Graham, I came in at 23hr 30min, and that was my limit, so approaching the Paddy I knew I had to get faster. My first Paddy was 25hr 45min, just before I got cancer. My second was 23hr 55min.

'I spent a lot of weekends there getting to know and love it. I love Wales and Scotland, but I live nearer to Wales!'

The Bob Graham – your highlights and lowlights

'I've always liked Dunmail to Wasdale, in either direction. It's a long section, and really important in the Round itself – whichever way to go, that's the crux leg. Five-and-a-half hours, and you'll start to feel quite rubbish on there...but if you can pull that around, by the next section you'll be on your way home.

'I'm less fond of the Langdales; they can be really tricky. I prefer to go clockwise. From Bowfell onwards is better. The bit I don't like is Skiddaw, Calva and Blencathra, either way round. Skiddaw is just a huge lump that's got to be climbed, and the weather can be really awful up there. The climb up the back of Blencathra goes on forever.

'The Helvellyn section is a bit fast and flat for me, and navigation in the dark is also very fiddly. People underestimate that section – you can go up on a sunny day and you can see everything and find the tops no problem, but that section is often run in the dark on the full Round, and the clag can hang around that ridge, and you can easily miss the paths and cairns and drop off one side or another.

'As for Broad Stand, I have a rope up except when it's wet, when I have said I won't go up that way. It's the slabs above rather than the first few steps for me – maybe they face into the rain, but they are lethal in the wet. You can lose as much time as you've just gained. If it's wet it's far better for me to go around by Foxes Tarn. That's an assessment on the day...and at least it saves you having someone hanging around with a rope.'

The Paddy Buckley – your highlights and lowlights

'You can tell by looking at the records that everyone finds the Paddy hard, and I think it's the rock. There's only so fast you can run over that rock, because you just can't stride out, you're always picking your way.

'I'm thinking of the Glyders in particular, but even the Boundary Ridge – the eastern section over the Moelwyns – it's pretty complex. It's a clever route – I like that Paddy has said you can start and finish wherever you want, but there isn't really an easy section on it.

'I make sure I'm not on the Glyders in the dark, ideally by being ahead of schedule. People often try to do the Snowdon section in the dark, but if you're ahead on that it's possible to end up trying to do Tryfan in the dark, which is not great.

'The first time I started at Nantmor, running clockwise – that was the way my running club, Dark Peak, used to do it. I wouldn't do that now, because of the Moelwyns. Doing it that way, you don't run very much on that leg because you are tired, and then you have some big climbs at the end. Even the long descent from Cnicht, you lose time because you are tired, you just can't pick your feet up.

'Now I prefer a Capel Curig start, others prefer Llanberis. The trouble with Capel is you tend to start at 10 or 11 in the morning. I generally like a pre-dawn start, but if you start at Llanberis at 2am, then you only have a few hours of darkness, which is less intimidating for some. From Llanberis also means you are still fresh when you are on the Glyders. But all that said, I still prefer starting at Capel, because the Boundary Ridge section is tough, and it goes a lot quicker if you are still fresh.

'The Nantmor section on the west of the route is a hard section – you look at it on the map and think it's a short leg, but there are some steep climbs and complicated exits off hills. And a lot of heather!

'I look forward to climbing up through the quarries after Llanberis. I like the quarries in the east too. You can just imagine all the people there

The Glyders, Paddy Buckley Round

The view from Stob Coire Bhealaich, near Spinks' ridge, Charlie Ramsay Round

working away, it's amazing. For the Dinorwig section, I just climb up the inclines rather than using the Foxes Path. It's possible just to use the road, too, since strictly speaking we're not supposed to be in there.

'To get up onto the Carneddau, I prefer Paddy's original route via the Afon Iloer. Going up the south ridge of Pen yr Ole Wen, there always seems to be rocks to climb or work around. I sometimes find the Carneddau a bit stressful – if you start from Capel then it's the end of the Round, it can be tricky in bad weather. But I like the descent off, it's just got enough of everything to keep your interest, and not too much road at the end.'

The Charlie Ramsay – your highlights and lowlights

'I did the Tranter anticlockwise, but I've done the Ramsay clockwise. I don't like going up the Ben, and don't really like coming off it either, so always glad to get that one out of the way first.

'I like the Grey Corries, and now that I've spent more time on it, I enjoy the further section around Loch Treig too, and linking those two up with the Easains is nice, because there aren't really paths, so you are finding your own way. That's the best part of the Ramsay really, being off trail. If you recce properly, there are some really great routes.

'The area between Chno Dearg and Beinn na Lap can be tricky – people seem to get it wrong quite often on their attempt, because it's miles from anywhere so maybe they've reconnoitred it less often, or in a rush. Aiming for the burn

between Chno Dearg and Meall Garbh seems to be a popular choice. There are amazing views off to the Ben Alder Munros from Beinn na Lap.

'Around Fersit, the railway people are sharp as hell – I've been shouted at, it's a delicate area, so one to be aware of.

'On the Mamores side, Binnein Mor is hard to reconnoitre because the snow is slow to melt. On Binnein Beag, I use the path on the south (east) side rather than the gully on the west (shown on the Harvey map).'

How do the Big Rounds compare to other big runs and races in the UK and Europe?

'I don't think they do. For a start, they aren't waymarked at all. Stats can be deceiving too – it's not just about ascent and distance.

'I have people contact me from London, asking if they can reconnoitre the Bob Graham online. The answer to that is **no**, in a word. Maybe if you are a really good navigator, then it might be possible to do the Round "on sight" but for most people who have done some ultras and live in cities without everyday access to the hills, then your chances of success are low to none.

'Folks coming from Europe are seeing the popularity of the Bob Graham and thinking "I've done the UTMB, I'll have a go", but they don't factor in the navigation, our weather, and the DIY aspect of the rounds – gathering people around for support and pacing, transport, the logistical side of things. It's totally different to any of the races I've done in Europe – there are no little flags to follow.

'In a race, you generally have 40 hours, but the 24 hours allowed for the Big Three does add another stress, too.'

What advice do you have for people thinking about a Round?

'Personally, I don't like it being part of a tick list, so just get up on the hills nearest to you, and think about whether it is really for you. With a race, you don't need to worry about the logistics until the final weeks beforehand, it's just on the training. Any one of the Big Three is the minimum of a full year's worth of preparation – driving up, reconnoitring in all weathers, and getting your pacers and supporters to do the same. It's a big commitment for everyone, and the Rounds deserve that, actually.

'You need to work out your own schedule – don't rely on someone else's. I don't publish mine online anymore because it doesn't do people any favours. A proper reconnoitre over several months means you can begin to work out what the pace should be over the full Round, decide your split times and then take that knowledge back with you on your training runs at home. You need to stop stopping! People stop for all sorts of reasons – to eat, drink, change socks. You need to get rid of all those minutes that you waste – that was key for me going from the Bob Graham into the Paddy Buckley.'

What role does your support play on the Big Rounds?

'The onus is always on the contender to navigate and be leading the attempt, but yes, of course support is invaluable. Sometimes it's about navigation and they might know a slightly better line than you do; sometimes it's morale – you are tired, sick, feeling out of it. It's equally important that all your pacers are 100% self-sufficient, know how to get themselves off the hill on their own, know the route themselves, and it should be expected that if they can't keep up they'll just get dropped.

'You need to support others to get support yourself. It's bad form to expect others to support you and then drop off the scene for others. You might get away with one Round that way, but long term for all three you won't find people will help you unless you help them. Diaries need to be cleared if they need the same in return. It's good training anyway.'

How did you start running?

'I joined Penistone Footpath Runners in my 30s, and the Bob Graham was a motivator – I just wanted to do it. I was on the mountains locally, and it sounded like my sort of challenge. I attempted it within about four years of starting running, and got round. My own supporters came from Penistone and Dark Peak Fell Runners, who join forces in the summer so a few people can attempt together. Being part of a network is a great help with logistics – car shares, advice, pacing and support.'

Are you competitive?

'Yes, with myself...and others if it's a race. If I've run properly, I've put so much in that I'll need to go to bed within about 30 minutes of finishing. We plan for it now – I'm a complete wreck, sometimes someone has to help me shower! That's why I had another go at the Bob Graham record, because I knew I could run faster than the 18 hours.'

What's special about the Big Three?

'You don't remember much of the Round attempts, because you're too busy concentrating on the schedules, eating, and support...but you do remember all the reconnoitres. It's getting to know your friends really well, having great memories of going round in all sorts of weather, and getting to know the area...because you stay in the area, spend money there and show your support for the place.

'Initially, the Rounds were a challenge – now I like to do a Round and a race per year, because they are so different. If I don't do a Round, I miss the "excuse" to go on the hills, the reason for a weekend away. I also like to do all the logistics myself, so partly it's a love of planning maybe... at the end of the day, I get a great team of people together, we're all really good friends, and we all help each other. It's really simple, and the complete opposite of the tick list mentality.'

Helene Whitaker

'Play to your strengths and mitigate your weaknesses'

Helene Whitaker (nee Diamantides) is a physiotherapist, distance runner and fell racer. In 1989, along with Adrian Belton, she was the first to complete all three Rounds in one summer. She became the first woman to complete the Ramsay, and set what was then the overall record for the Paddy Buckley in the same season (beating Adrian's time by two hours). They ran the final leg of their Bob Graham together, with Helene setting a new women's record for that too, at the time. She also won the first Dragon's Back Race in 1982, running with Martin Stone, a race so brutal it was not revived until 2012.

Helene has competed hard and very successfully – at home in the KIMM, Borrowdale, Wasdale Fell Race and the Langdale Horseshoe races (where she held the course record from 1982 to 2016!), and around the world. Alongside Alison Wright, she held the record for the Kathmandu to Everest base camp run for many decades.

Which Round was the most difficult for you?

'The Charlie Ramsay is a tough route. Both as a runner, and for supporters. Big hills, rough ground and dodgy weather with travel logistics are frequently an issue. And logistics are especially difficult for any support on the Ramsay – it seems to be an ideal circuit to do with minimal support. I did some of the hills for the first time on my own Charlie Ramsay, navigating and running with Mark Rigby for one-third of it on our own. He completed with me. The two of us ran around, we had two supporters, and then went home. Perfect! But without a doubt the most physically demanding for me.'

How do the Big Three compare to other ultra-distance challenges?

'Trail running is a "controlled environment" compared to the three Rounds, although it is possible to control your experience to a greater or lesser extent on rounds depending on your ethos: How well will you know your route? Are you using a GPS? How many pacers are with you, and how well do you know them, and they know the route?'

What advice can you give regarding route planning and reconnoitring?

'Know what you are letting yourself in for and prepare accordingly. For my solo Bob Graham, I carried a bivi bag in case of injury (no mobile phones in those days...). However, it is possible to over-reconnoitre and really put yourself off. It always seems impossible to meet times on a recce.

'I'd also say play to your strengths and mitigate your weaknesses. I hated the 3–4am spot and preferred not to run into a second night, so I tried to start at times when I would avoid doing so."

And food?

'I can always eat but a variety of savoury as well as sweet is important. Change textures. Check what happens when you eat food and then run with it in your stomach to see if it re-appears.'

What about putting a pacing team together?

'You are looking for appropriate ability, and the appropriate character for the point in the Round where you will need chat, cheer, silence or supportiveness. It takes time to work this all out!'

Helene Whitaker and Jim Mann on the
Dragon's Back Race © Rob Howard / Berghaus

Jasmin Paris

'It's about the sense of freedom'

Jasmin is a small animal vet for the University of Edinburgh, and a fell and sky runner. She is the current (overall) record holder for the Ramsay Round, and holds the women's record for both the Bob Graham and Paddy Buckley Rounds, all set in 2016. She is currently the fastest person on the Big Three with a cumulative time of 50hr 9min. In the same year, she won both the Tromso Skyrace and the Glen Coe Skyline, making her champion of the extreme series of the 2016 Skyrunner World Series.

Jasmin Paris on the Wasdale race

Which is your favourite of the three Rounds, and why?

'It depends whether I consider my experience whilst running them, or whether I try to take an unbiased view. For the Paddy Buckley I was tired almost from the start, which meant that I suffered. Nevertheless, the Paddy Buckley route was very beautiful, and wilder than I had imagined it would be.

'For the Bob Graham, I was fit and fresh, which definitely made it more enjoyable. The Ramsay was special because it was my "local" round, and I ran it intending, and succeeding, to get the overall record. The Ramsay Round is also the most remote of the three, and in real mountains, with big climbs. Overall, I'd probably have to say the Ramsay is my favourite, for the moment.'

Which was the most difficult for you?

'The Paddy Buckley, without a doubt. Not only were my legs already tired when I started (courtesy of a year of racing/ultra-running), but I was also limited in terms of daylight (I wanted to do all three Rounds in a year, so the Paddy was squeezed in during October), and the ground was waterlogged, which made the Boundary leg (Capel Curig to Nantmor) particularly challenging.'

Do you have any words of advice for those taking on the three Rounds?

'Don't set off in bad weather.

'Continuing the above point, I would advise planning support for two or three consecutive weekends. This way, you will not be tempted to set off in bad weather, just because you don't want to waste your opportunity for support.

'Go hiking in big mountains – I think this is the ideal preparation for these sorts of challenges. You need long days out with less risk of injury than running, lots of ascent and descent, and some altitude training.

'Reconnoitre the route if you don't already know the area – I didn't do the Paddy Buckley justice in that regard. Although that doesn't mean reconnoitre it to death! Keep in mind that repeated runs do have an impact (as can be easily seen on the Bob Graham) and by doing these Rounds it becomes part of our obligation to preserve the environment as well as the challenge for others in the future.

'Have good support, but no more than you need. "Good" in this context means people who

Jasmin Paris and pacers Finlay Wild and Jon Gay at the start of leg 3 (of her record breaking Charlie Ramsay Round)

know the way, and who you enjoy spending time with.

'Keep eating – it's really just a case of eating and putting one foot in front of the other.'

Any advice for each Round in particular?

'Of the three, the Bob Graham probably has the easiest terrain and the most trods. Getting support is easier, and you will meet more people on the Bob Graham than on the Welsh or the Scottish Rounds, including other people attempting a Bob Graham themselves, and those who might want to try the others in the future. So, it's a good place to start. Road support is also easy.

'The Ramsay is the most remote, and road support is limited to one point, which requires a walk in. Supporters who know the route are more limited, and they will need to walk or run in and out of the changeover points (except for the middle leg). The climbs are fewer, but are more serious.

'I'd say that for the Welsh Round, more so than for the other two, local knowledge or prior reconnoitring is essential, but as on the Ramsay, supporters who know the route are less plentiful than for the Bob Graham. The route is difficult to navigate in places (I'm thinking particularly of the Capel-Nantmor leg) and there are many subtle summits! It may be worth considering doing early in the season to avoid deep bracken. But, road support is very easy, and has the least amount of driving between the four points.'

Why hill run?

'I fell run primarily for the joy of being in the hills – I've always loved the outdoors, the wilder the better. It's about the sense of freedom too, moving fast over varied and challenging terrain. Plus, it's a pretty good way of keeping fit!'

Are you competing against the clock, yourself or your peers? Why compete at all?

'A bit of all the above. I am definitely competitive; I can't pretend I'm not...That said, I don't think it's all about winning – I think I recognise when I've given it everything, and can be proud of myself for that. If you ask why I compete, I think it's as much for the social side of it as the racing itself. Fell running is an incredibly friendly sport, and I'm proud to be a part of it.'

Jim Mann

'Big, fun hill days. It's as simple as that'

Jim runs a birch syrup company, and is the record holder for all three of the Rounds in winter. He set the new best times for both the Paddy Buckley and the Charlie Ramsay within a month over the winter of 2017. He also ran one of the fastest times for a winter Round of the Bob Graham in the same month, but didn't manage to better his own previous record, set in 2013. He is still only the second person (after Adrian Belton) to run all three under 24 hours within a calendar month, and the first to do so in winter. In 2017, he set a new record for the most (30!) Munros in 24 hours, in the Cairngorms. His favourite of the Big Three is the Ramsay.

Jim Mann, in Inverness

What got you started in hill running?

'I ran cross country at school in Lancashire, wanted something to do at half term, and did the Pendle race – I was about 13. The simplicity of hill running really appealed to me then, as it does now. I kept running until Uni', had 15 years out, and started again aged about 33, when I had a now or never moment I guess. The running was always here and there, but I wasn't training. I've always had to train really hard. I'm not natural at all. It took me about three years to get some fitness back, so that I could run six or seven days a week. After that I started training, and built it to the level I'm at now. It just takes time and hard work.'

What's the story behind your first winter Round?

'I did my first Bob Graham in September 2010, after about a year of racing to get fit and supporting others on their attempts. My time was 22hr 08min, and the record for winter at the time was 22hr 06min. The summer Round hadn't tested me like I thought it would, and I'm one of these people that doesn't want it easy...so I thought I'd have a go at a winter one.

'The first one I tried, I'd set a date, rather than waiting for weather – there are still people making that mistake – and it was blizzard conditions. I didn't get round. I came back at the end of the winter window, got a really nice day, and got the winter record. In 2013, I went back to try and run it faster, and ran it in 18hr 18min, a new record. My third one, I ran just to get all three done within a winter month, and it was in gale force winds.'

Can you talk about what's classed as a winter Round?

'The classification for a winter Round is quite arbitrary – it's a timeframe, not about the conditions. I've never run what's called a 'mid-winter' Bob Graham, and I've never done one in full snow conditions either.

'Whatever the conditions, running a Round in winter is still a huge achievement – but people need to be transparent about those conditions. Sponsorship and the media are starting to have an impact on the way people describe what they are doing. That isn't my sport. My sport is paying £2.50 to run up a mountain and come back down again for my pie...and maybe a pint if I could get my age under the radar!'

In what general ways do the Rounds differ under winter conditions as compared to summer?

'Winter is just so much more committing. Most hill runners won't have come through winter mountaineering, but you need that skillset and that mindset. Something like Jon Gay's first sub 24-hour Ramsay, that's a really special combination of skills. He was running on frozen neve – conditions he'd waited years for. Some of the runouts in winter are really extreme.

'One of the things I learnt through doing winter recces on the Bob Graham was you don't know which route option you are going to use until the day. Something might be iced up, or banked out and impassable, so you need to have alternatives ready. And you need to know all your escape routes in winter conditions, too. Your choices depend on the conditions on the day itself. You can still get your choices wrong, so you also need the skills to be able back off on a route option...or ultimately back off on an attempt altogether. You may be postholing, wading through drifts, front pointing over icy slopes or managing changing wind direction or avalanche risk. That's the exciting part of it too, of course. You just never know what you are going to get. 24 hours is a long time in winter; the conditions can change completely over the course of an attempt.

'Planning for a winter Round requires watching for a stable 24-hour weather window. I reckon we get two per season on the west side of the country, and typically you'll see them coming. I use www.windy.com and www.xcweather.co.uk for windspeed in particular, and the BBC mountain forecast is pretty good too. But long-range winter forecasting is really fickle.

'A winter Ramsay in particular is far more dangerous, partly because it's so remote. They aren't going to get in to rescue you from those mountains in time if the weather flips. For the group I run with, rescue is our very last resort. Our attitude is you can take calculated risks for yourself, but not for others. The other rule I have is for anyone who comes out on a winter Round – I want to know they can get themselves off the hill on their own. And lastly, in winter I always carry my own survival kit – bivi bag, full waterproofs and emergency food. In the event that I'm separated from my support, I want to be sure I have the bare minimum to keep me alive.

'Another thing to bear in mind is that on the high ground, you will inevitably be moving slower than in summer, because you need to keep safe. Of course, we use running crampons (not microspikes) and a lightweight ice axe, but the balancing act is to keep safe while also moving at a pace that keeps you warm and gets you round in time.'

What about pacer support on a winter Round?

'I've been lucky to have really serious people around me for the winter Rounds: Graham Nash, Jon Ascroft, Jasmin Paris, Konrad Rawlik, Shane Ohly – winter climbers, mountaineers, mountain leaders as well as runners. They're not just quick; they have a really wide range of skills between them and a huge amount of experience, and they're all better winter mountaineers than I am. They are also people I run with on a regular basis, so we know each other's strengths and limitations. That's important for any Round attempt, but the pool of people for a winter Round is inevitably much smaller.

'I don't want to be the person to say, "don't try this" – because that's too much of a temptation to some – but most people really should not be doing winter Rounds. I'm not just saying that out of ego – to be honest, I probably shouldn't have done the winter Ramsay, save for the people I had around me. I could do support for a single leg, sure – but after 18 hours, your judgement becomes impaired, and you can end up relying on those people too much. I questioned the conditions on the last leg of my winter Paddy, too.

Winter recce'ing, Loch Treig

The Mamores from Stob Coire Easian

'If people try to do the Rounds in winter without doing the preparation, then people will die – and you can end up killing somebody else along with you. It's "cool" and "fun" to try these things, sure, but don't do it because you want to say you've done it. The entire team need to be operating at a really high level to make the risks remotely manageable.'

How do you train for these winter Rounds, given that conditions in the UK are so variable?

'Get "fell-hard"; stay out in all weathers, get used to navigating in the dark and in a blizzard. I sometimes go looking for bad weather just to challenge myself. You need to push yourself towards your limits.'

How are you fuelling on a winter Round?

'I don't break stride at road crossings – I switch pacers and take on fuel, but on the move. There's no benefit to stopping for me, I'd get cold and stiffen up. I just want it done and to get to the pub!

'On the Ramsay it's harder to fuel, because there are only two chances to get hot food as opposed to four.

'I drink stream water, not energy drinks. In winter, the support will carry water if the streams and burns are frozen over. For food, I swear by 4-for-£1 chocolate bars. And I usually have cup-a-soup style pastas brewed up very liquidly so I can drink rather than eat them, and a cup of coffee. Fruit in syrup goes down well, or maybe rice pudding (as long as I don't have to carry it – a pack exploded in my bag once and killed a mobile phone!). I use paper cups, so I can crush the cups and stow them away easily after I've drunk the liquids.

'If I'm in a mess then gels are OK, but I need to follow it with something, or better still eat before, to avoid the peak-trough effect.

'The most important thing is; can you stomach it? You need to be able to get it down, whether you want to eat or not. Take something that you like. If I'm supporting then I force people to eat to the very end. The Bob Graham is the worst for that; on that 5-mile run-in people forget to fuel, because they are running on adrenalin.'

Looking at each of the Rounds in turn, where are the problem areas for a winter attempt?

Bob Graham Round

'Going clockwise, on leg 1: if you get problems on Skiddaw it's usually deep snow on the north side. The real issue for leg 1 is coming off Blencathra. There are four options for runners; Doddick Fell is the best route if it's icy, it's a gentler incline. Hall's Fell can be nasty under ice. Then there's "the parachute descent" onto Middle Tongue, which people have had to be helicoptered off from! The last is to take a line onto the start of the parachute, and then cut back into Hall's Fell after the steeper section. It all depends where the wind has blown the snow. This all needs looking at properly under lots of different winter conditions, so you know what you can work with if you are silly enough to be trying at all!

'For leg 2, snow can accumulate on the northeast of Fairfield. There's also the steepening ground between Lower Man and Helvellyn, which cornices very easily. The temptation is to take a straight-line bearing between the two hills, and the danger is dropping through onto the cliffs above Brown Cove. People die every year there. Most people are doing this in the dark (because the daylight section for a winter Round is usually between Rossett Pike and Great Gable or thereabouts) so it's an easy mistake to make.

'You also have to watch leg 2 for water – if it's frozen, there's nothing on the ridge until you drop down the spring at Grisedale tarn.

'For leg 3, the west face of Bowfell wind crusts really easily, and the slope below is steep and full of boulders. It can be in lethal condition when everything else to that point has been benign. Getting up to the top of Broad Crag can be tricky, too. It's easy to break a leg by slipping on ice or going through snow covered boulders.

'Scafell is the crux in winter, as in summer. I won't use Broad Stand in winter. Lord's Rake, on its own or in combination with the West Wall traverse can work, but I have lost an hour in there, picking my way through. My preferred winter route is usually Foxes Tarn. You lose a bit of height but it's simple and safer, although there have been rockfalls in there as well. There really isn't a safe route here in winter – you are mitigating risk.'

The Paddy Buckley Round

'From Capel Curig, going clockwise on leg 1: there are no real issues until the Moelwyns. The straight line that runners take down to the quarry before Foel Dhu can get icy; you'll need an axe, and there are holes. Nicky's route goes around (similar to the one described in the route description).

'The north face of Moelwyn Mawr can freeze so solid that an axe won't penetrate, so it's a good idea to come even further east than feels right, to avoid sliding down that slope and hitting the wire fence at the bottom.

'On leg 2, the steep descent of Hebog can ice up. The scrambly descent on the Nantlle ridge will slow you down if the boulders are icy, but the potential for a serious fall is relatively low. It's certainly possible to break a leg in there, though.

'For leg 3, the final climb to Snowdon might give cause for concern, but usually it's fairly well trodden, even in winter. Coming off the back of Crib y Ddysgl can become very wind scoured and slippery, and it's quite a long and exposed descent, so that is an area to watch.

'On leg 4, the faint trods on Elidir Fawr can disappear under snow and ice, so it's easy to lose time there. The climb up onto the Glyder plateau can be really energy sapping under snow, and getting to the summit of Glyder Fach is very treacherous underfoot in the snow and ice. I've not had an issue with a descent of the Glyders personally; it's a broad gully and seems to collect snow and ice. And with Tryfan, again just watch out for gaps covered with snow.

'For leg 5, all of the Carneddau catches the wind and the snow. It can get pretty nasty and you stay high for a long time, so it's quite committing. The scramble descent at Bwlch Eryl Farchog has also caught me out before in winter – trying to find purchase with tired legs!'

The Ramsay Round

'It's definitely the most serious in winter – the highest and the most remote. Going anticlockwise on leg 1, the first serious hotspot is the descent of Binnein Mor. It's a big hill, and the northern coire catches a lot of snow which can ice up. I face in and front point down the eastern side of the north spur of the coire.

'Going into the valley section after the long decent NE from Sgùrr Èilde Mòr, I look to drop east off the ridge just south of a spot height marked 680m, aiming for a footbridge on the path between Luibeilt and the loch – that's my support point. But, the crags to the south of that spot height hold snow and ice, so that's another flashpoint to be avoided.

'On leg 2, I've not had any issues, personally. But leg 3 makes up for it in spades.

'The Grey Corries are really steep, and the potential for slipping off or falling through a cornice is high. The ridge ascent of Sgùrr Chòinnich Mòr can be quite serious as well. If there's enough snow it can bank out, so care needs to be taken there.

'For the climb onto the Aonachs, I've used Charlie's Gully, which is about the limit of what I feel comfortable on in winter. I wouldn't use Spinks' Ridge in winter; it's too exposed higher up. If neither of those appeal, then there's usually a way through, south of the gully. This is the equivalent of Broad Stand on the Bob Graham – there is no entirely safe way.

'Once onto the Aonachs, you are really exposed, and then finding the descent to the *bealach* is rocky and very steep, dangerous ground that ices up easily. The cairn marking the top of the descent also disappears under snow.

'You won't get lost on the ridge of the CMD, but it can be icy. Once on the arête, you may need to stay right on top, as the chicken run paths will often be banked out and unusable.

'After all that, the Ben can be relatively benign. In summer, you have to stick to the path because of the erosion on the hill, but in winter you can take a much more direct line once off the summit plateau.'

Do you run competitively, and if so, why?

'Yes I am competitive – I do get fired up by it. But in the end, all this is just a bunch of mates going out for a big day in the hills and having fun. That's the roots of it, and that's what I love. It's no different to people going hillwalking for the day, doing one-tenth of the distance; you have a day that wears you out, and you land up in the pub...which is exactly where the Cairngorms Munro record finished (see Appendix D). Big, fun hill days. It's as simple as that.'

Mike Hartley

'Running is just the vehicle'

Mike holds the record for the fastest Pennine Way (2 days, 17 hours and 20 minutes), which he achieved in July 1989. A year later he ran the Big Three Rounds back to back, travelling by car in between. His total time was 3 days, 14 hours and 20 minutes (including transit), with the Ramsay at 21hr 14min, the Bob Graham at 23hr 48min, and the Paddy Buckley at 33hr 30min. This achievement has yet to be repeated, despite some serious challenges.

How did you get started, and how did it evolve to endurance running?

'I started running in 1980 at the age of 28. I came from fell walking and rock climbing while at school. A year later I caught the marathon bug and couldn't get enough of it. In 1988, I joined Cannock and Stafford Athletic Club, which allowed me to develop by training and racing specifically for speed.

'By then, I'd completed the Bob Graham Round twice and the Fellsman Hike six times, placing first on two occasions. In 1986, I won the West Highland Way Race and in 1987, the Fellsman and LDWA 100 on consecutive weekends. I'd also had a taste of the really long stuff, completing the Tan Hill to Cat and Fiddle (120 miles) in 1986 and the Southern Upland Way (212 miles) in 1988.'

Mike Hartley on Yewbarrow © Mike Hartley collection

Mike Hartley and pacer Howard Sawyer on Helvellyn © Mike Hartley collection

Tell us about the Pennine Way record

'1989 was to be the year. I'd found the Southern Upland Way tough – and I mean tough: blisters, extreme stiffness, hallucinations, the lot. To succeed, I knew I'd have to raise my game. My diary shows a mixture of high mileage weeks interspersed with injuries and visits to the physio, often cycling to maintain fitness when I was unable to run. To prepare, I did 14 weeks at more than 100 miles per week with a maximum of 130 miles. In the spring I reduced my weekly mileage but took on regular long (and sometimes record-breaking) runs, roughly a month apart.

'I'd gone through two nights without sleep on the Southern Upland Way, so I intended to do the same for the Pennine Way. And I planned a schedule with a decreasing pace.'

Were the Big Rounds back-to-back inevitable after that?

'I didn't think about the Three Rounds until after I'd completed the Pennine Way, so I didn't consider it as a preparation, but of course it was. By the time I tried for it, I'd done the BGR three times in under 24 hours. I'd not done the Ramsay or the Paddy Buckley before, but I had done a lot of support, training and reconnoitring on those hills.

'I don't think anything could have prepared me for the Big Rounds back to back, but it must have helped psychologically. It was more about seeking out that level of endeavour that I suppose I've always wanted to find. I wrote at the time that I wanted to be in no doubt where my limits lay.

'When I first finished it, I really wasn't sure if was worth all the pain and effort. I wondered if I'd just done it for the sake of it. Looking back now, I think it was significant and well worth doing.'

Are you competitive?

'I've never really felt that way; it's just that I've always wanted to achieve as much as I can. And running is just the vehicle – any sport could give the same rewards and experiences.'

Keri Wallace

'You don't need to be super-human'

Keri is a journalist and fell runner, and runs a guiding company for female trail runners in Lochaber. Her experience of the Big Rounds was as a continuous, consecutive journey over several days, but not on the clock as such.

How did you decide on the Big Rounds as a continuous journey?

'I devised my challenge following many years of battling with a reoccurring knee injury that prevented me from running. It was a way of setting myself a goal that would be a stretch for me physically and mentally, would require commitment, stamina and planning – but wouldn't hurt my knee. I decided that I would walk the three mountain Rounds back to back, as multi-day journeys. I would have one travel day between each, moving between countries. I aimed to raise money for charity and wanted to do it solo.'

How did you prepare for all three in a row?

'I walked and jogged 338 miles in training over four months to prepare and was delighted to find that the low impact strength training actually cured my knee of injury. Gradually, I was able to run whole legs during reconnoitres, which meant I could travel (reasonably) fast and light through the mountains, rather than carry an overnight pack. The thought of a fully unsupported challenge appealed to me, but doing the Rounds as a multi-day push would have meant carrying a lot of equipment.'

Keri Wallace on the Ring of Steall Skyrace © Oriol Batista

What support did you have on your challenge?

'I started each Round at a point that best fitted my plan, rather than the classic locations, and I broke each round into three or four sections, starting and finishing at the roadside where possible. If I was staying in a B&B, each morning I would get a lift back to the point where I had left the route the previous day and continue. My parents met me at the end of each day in England and Wales, and friends supported me in Scotland by hiking into bothies with food and firewood. It was great to stay in historic pubs like the Wasdale Head Inn and the Pen-Y-Gwryd hotel – plenty of local flavour combined with a rich mountaineering history.

'I didn't have any pacers on the Rounds, as I was only looking to complete my challenge, as opposed to achieving any particular time. I'm actually very competitive, both with myself and others, but these Rounds brought out a different side of me, something that I approached without rushing or racing in mind. I was seeking a journey and an adventure.'

How much of the route did you know beforehand?

'I knew some sections of the three Rounds pretty well, but didn't know how they all fitted together. I probably reconnoitred two-thirds of each Round in training, leaving some for 'interest' during the event. This proved to be a bad idea; in very poor weather the new terrain and navigation slowed my progress and was unsettling.'

What was challenging?

'Pre-booking accommodation and annual leave from work meant that when the weather forecast turned bad, I had to just carry on and overcome! I met very poor visibility and hail in Wales, storm force winds in the Lake District, and gales and blizzards in Scotland. Energy, navigation and moving over technical ground were all manageable by comparison.

'On my Bob Graham, I took a day off to avoid strong winds, combining two legs into a single day to keep to my schedule. On my third day, I ran from Threlkeld to Wasdale (30 miles) to finish the Round as planned.

'On the Ramsay, the weather was also unkind. On day three, in blizzard conditions on the Aonachs, I made the very difficult decision to abort. It was unsafe to traverse the CMD arête, especially solo. I was devastated after coming so far, but feel confident that I made a sound decision.'

What did you learn from the experience?

'After doing the Big Rounds in one go, my view of what constituted a "big day in the hills" fundamentally changed. Anyone thinking of tackling these three Rounds should not to be intimidated by the size of the challenge. Breaking these Rounds into bite-sized chunks mean that they can be done by any fit and capable hillgoer. You don't need to be a super-human fell-runner. My times were:

- Bob Graham Round – 26hr 6min (over three days)
- Paddy Buckley Round – 34hr 42min (over four days)
- Charlie Ramsay Round – (minus two summits!) – 25hr 37min (over three days)

'Reconnoitre well, make sure your navigation skills (map and compass) are up to scratch, and do enough training to make sure the distance and ascent is achievable for you.

'If you are able to be flexible with regards to the date of your adventure, then you'll be best placed to avoid bad weather and potentially dangerous conditions. I would not recommend anyone pressing on to achieve a goal or challenge at all costs. As a Mountain Rescue Team member, I still decided that it was safest to turn back – right at the very end. The most important thing really is the journey, not the final goal itself.'

An early morning inversion over the Aonachs from the east ridge of Càrn Mòr Dearg, the Ramsay Round

The quarry track above Llyn Stwlan (leg 1, Paddy Buckley Round)

APPENDIX A
Hills and their heights

Bob Graham Round

Leg 1: The Moot Hall, Keswick: start and finish
Skiddaw 931m | Great Calva 690m | Blencathra 898m

Leg 2: Threlkeld
Clough Head 726m | Great Dodd 857m | Watson's Dodd 789m | Stybarrow Dodd 843m | Raise 883m | White Side 863m | Lower Man 925m | Helvellyn 950m | Nethermost Pike 891m | Dollywagon Pike 858m | Fairfield 873m | Seat Sandal 736m

Leg 3: Dunmail Raise
Steel Fell 553m | Calf Crag 537m | Sergeant Man 736m | High Raise 762m | Thunacar Knott 723m | Harrison Stickle 736m | Pike O' Stickle 709m | Rossett Pike 651m | Bowfell 903m | Esk Pike 885m | Great End 907m | Ill Crag 930m | Broad Crag 934m | Scafell Pike 978m | Scafell 964m

Leg 4: Wasdale Campsite
Yewbarrow 628m | Red Pike 826m | Steeple 819m | Pillar 892m | Kirk Fell 802m | Great Gable 899m | Green Gable 801m | Brandreth 715m | Grey Knotts 697m

Leg 5: Honister Pass
Dale Head 753m | Hindscarth 727m | Robinson 737m

Paddy Buckley Round

Leg 1: Capel Curig start and finish
(note that this round can begin from any point – see Rules for runners)
Carnedd Moel Siabod 872m | Clogwyn Bwlch y Maen 548m | Carnedd Y Cribau 591m | Cerrig Cochion 550m | Moel Meirch 607m | Ysgafell Wen 650m | Mynydd Llynnau'r Cwn 669m | Unnamed Summit aka 'Three Tops' 672m | Moel Druman 676m | Allt Fawr 698m | Foel Ddu 458m | Moel yr hydd 648m | Moelwyn Bach 710m | Craig Ysgafn 689m | Moelwyn Mawr 770m | Cnicht 689m

Leg 2: Nantmor/Aberglaslyn
Bryn Banog 520m | Moel Hebog 782m | Moel yr Ogof 655m | Moel Lefn 638m | Y Gyrn 452m | Mynydd y Ddwy Elor 466m | Trum y Ddysgl 709m | Mynydd Drws-y-Coed 695m | Y Garn 633m

Leg 3: Pont Cae'r Gors/Rhyd-Ddu
Craig Wen 608m | Yr Aran 747m | Cribau Tregalan 931m | Snowdon 1085m | Crib y Ddysgl 1065m | Moel Cynghorion 674m | Foel Goch 605m | Foel Gron 629m | Moel Eilio 726m

Leg 4: Llanberis
Elidir Fach 795m | Elidir Fawr 924m | Mynydd Perfedd 812m | Foel-goch 831m | Y Garn 947m | Glyder Fawr 999m | Glyder Fach 994m | Tryfan 917m

Heading to camp under An Gearanach

Leg 5: Ogwen Cottage/Gwern Gof Uchaf

Pen yr Ole Wen 978m | Carnedd Dafydd 1044m | Carnedd Llewelyn 1064m | Pen yr Helgi Du 833m |
Pen Llithrig y Wrach 799m

Charlie Ramsay Round

Leg 1: Glen Nevis YHA: start and finish

Mullach nan Coirean 939m | Stob Ban 999m | Sgùrr a' Mhàim 1099m | Sgòr an Iubhair 1001m |
Am Bodach 1032m | Stob Choire a' Chàirn 981m | An Gearanach 982m | Na Gruagaichean 1056m |
Binnein Mòr 1130m | Binnein Beag 943m | Sgùrr Èilde Mòr 1010m

Leg 2: vicinity of Loch Èilde Mòr or Luibeilt

Beinn na Lap 935m | Chno Dearg 1046m | Stob Coire Sgriodain 979m

Leg 3: Fersit

Stob a' Coire Mheadhoin 1105m | Stob Coire Easain 1115m | Stob Ban 977m | Stob Choire Claurigh
1177m | Stob Coire an Laoigh 1116m | Sgùrr Chòinnich Mòr 1094m | Aonach Beag 1234m |
Aonach Mòr 1221m | Càrn Mòr Dearg 1220m | Ben Nevis 1344m

APPENDIX B

Distance and elevation at a glance

All figures are approximate and depend on the line taken.

Bob Graham Round

Leg	Distance	Elevation
1	12.3 miles (19.8km)	5272ft (1610m)
2	13.4 miles (21.5km)	5895ft (1800m)
3	14.9 miles (24km)	6833ft (2080m)
4	10.4 miles (16.7km)	6167ft (1880m)
5	10.5 miles (16.8km)	2611ft (800m)
Total	61.4 miles (98.8km)	26,778ft (8160m)

Paddy Buckley Round

Leg	Distance	Elevation
1	21.3 miles (34.2km)	7568ft (2310m)
2	9.7 miles (15.6km)	5275ft (1610m)
3	11.8 miles (19km)	6217ft (1900m)
4	9.5 miles (15.3km)	5711ft (1740m)
5	10.2 miles (16.4km)	3979ft (1210m)
Total	62.4 miles (100.5km)	28,750ft (8700m)

Charlie Ramsay Round

Leg	Distance	Elevation
1	22.1 miles (35.6km)	11,610ft (3540m)
2	14.6 miles (23.5km)	4891ft (1490m)
3	20.9 miles (33.7km)	12,378ft (3770m)
Total	57.6 miles (92.8km)	28,879ft (8800m)

APPENDIX C

Firsts on the Rounds

First
Bob Graham in 1932, Charlie Ramsay in 1978. The Paddy Buckley Round was first completed by Wendy Dodds in 1982.

First women
Bob Graham Round: Jean Dawes, 1977.
Paddy Buckley Round: Wendy Dodds, 1982.
Charlie Ramsay Round: Helene Diamantides, 1989.

Big Three
The first to do the three Rounds, each within 24 hours was Martin Stone, in 1987. Martin was also the first repeat on the Ramsay (in that same year) and the first within 24 hours on the Buckley (1985). It's likely that he is also the only person ever to have completed the three Rounds solo and unsupported.

The first to do all three in one season is jointly held by Adrian Belton and Helene Diamantides (1989).

Helene was also the first woman to do all three Rounds, in that same year.

The first to do all three consecutively (driving between the three) was the one and only Mike Hartley, in 1990. His times were: Charlie Ramsay – 21hr 14min; Bob Graham – 23hr 48min; Paddy Buckley – 33hr 30min.

First in winter
Bob Graham Round: Jon Brockbank, 1986
Paddy Buckley Round: Martin Stone, 1989
Charlie Ramsay Round: Jon Gay, 2013
The first person to complete all of the Big Three in winter (as well as summer) was Tom Philips.

For up to date 'bests', please refer to Tony Wimbush's excellent resource: www.gofar.org.uk.

APPENDIX D

Round extensions, and other eye-wateringly long challenges

As we've seen, extending the number of hills on the Rounds as they currently exist is built into the DNA of hill-running challenges. All three Rounds have been extended, the current records standing at 77 for the Bob Graham, set by Mark Hartell; 28 for the Ramsay (now 27, after a Munro was declassified) held by Adrian Belton; and 51 for the Buckley, set by the same Adrian Belton.

To give a sense of just how far (and fast) people are prepared to go, the record for all 214 of Wainwright's Lakeland fells is currently held by Steve Birkenshaw. He took 6 days and 13 hours,

beating Joss Naylor's previous record of 7 days, 1 hour and 25 minutes.

The record for the double Bob Graham is currently held by Nicky Spinks (43hr 30min), set in 2016. Nicky was the first woman and the second person to achieve this in under 48 hours, (and fourth overall – in 1977, Boyd Millen was the first person to ever complete the double (52hr 30min); Roger Baumeister was next in 1979 (46hr 36min); and Eric Draper was third, in 1995 (50hr 35min)).

Nicky is currently the only person to have run all three Rounds as doubles. She followed her double Bob Graham with a double Ramsay's Round in 2018 in a time of 56hr, 56min, and a double Paddy Buckley Round in 2019, in a time of 57hr, 27min. Like the definitions of winter conditions, what constitutes a double round is the subject of much discussion and debate.

There are dozens of other routes not based on the Big Rounds – a look at the gofar website or John Fleetwood's blog (see Appendix E) will furnish you plenty of ideas and demonstrate that imagination is only limited by fitness and stamina.

Most Munros
In Scotland, there's a long tradition of the 'most Munros in 24 hours' challenge, which was first set by Philip Tranter, in Lochaber in 1964.

The Rigby Round
All of the high ground in the northern Cairngorms was first run by Mark Rigby in 1988 in a time of 22hr 44min. He ran across 17 Munros, 75 miles and 19,000ft (5791.2m) of ascent. The summit of Sgòr an Lochain Uaine has since been promoted to Munro status, making this an 18 Munro, sub 24-hour challenge. Mark set out with something different in mind: solo, unsupported and un-reconnoitred; 'the antithesis of the trend towards down-to-the-minute planning'.

The Broxap Round
Pushing the 24-hour hill runners tally past mere fitness and into the realms of the experimental pain management, Jon Broxap successfully completed his 28 Munro record in 1988, in a time of 23hr 20min. Beginning at the Cluanie Inn in Glen Shiel, he circuited Glen Shiel via the South Cluanie Ridge and the Five Sisters of Kintail before running north to Beinn Fhada and onto the tops north of Glen Affric. This was a staggering 78 miles and more than 33,000ft (10058.4m) of ascent.

The Phil Clarke Round
Attempts to move beyond this record were unsuccessful until 2017. In 1997, Adrian Belton bolted on an additional four to Ramsay's 24, whilst in 2008 Steve Pyke tried for a mind boggling 31 Munros in the Glen Shiel area by including the hills south of Loch Mullardoch. Sadly, he 'only' managed 20 before foul weather forced him to

abort his attempt. The reclassification of Munros has since increased the Broxap Round to 29 and reduced Belton's extension to 27 without either of them running the routes again!

In 2017, Jim Mann ran a frankly ridiculous 30 Munros covering Glenshee, Lochnagar and the northern Cairngorms, which he named the Phil Clarke Round after the 1990 winner of the KIMM (now the OMM) and one of the first repeaters of Rigby's Round. Mann and his support managed a time of 22hr 05min, which meant they had time to go to the pub afterwards.

A new benchmark was set – 30 Munros and at least 1 pint within 24 hours. Beat that!

What about the other two?
It turns out this book should have been called The Big Five Rounds. Just when I thought it was safe, there are also the two 24-hour rounds west over the water. These are the newest Rounds and yet more proof that hill running innovation continues apace:

In County Wicklow, Ireland, the Wicklow Round (www.imra.ie/wicklowround) covers 26 peaks, more than 100km and 19,685ft (6000m) of ascent. It was first run within 24 hours in 2009 by Moire O' Sullivan, whose book is listed in Appendix E.

In County Down, Northern Ireland, there's the Denis Rankin Round (www.denisrankinround.com), named after the pioneering hill runner. It covers more than 90km and 21,325ft (6498.8m) of ascent, visiting all the hills over 400m in the Mournes. It was first run within 24 hours in 2014 by Billy Reed.

On 13 May 2018, John Ryan – supported by Carnethy AC and others – finished his Ramsay Round, and became the first and only person to that date to have completed all of the Big Five Rounds in under 24 hours.

APPENDIX E

Further reading and viewing

Online

Perhaps the definitive web guide to long-distance running challenges: www.gofar.org.uk

The Bob Graham 24 Hour Club members' website: www.bobgrahamclub.org.uk

Charlie Ramsay's website: www.ramsaysround.co.uk

Bob Wightman is the membership secretary for the Bob Graham Club and his website includes some useful tools for runners on timed attempts, as well as some basic route notes: www.bobwightman.co.uk/run/index.php

Nicky Spinks' website: www.runbg.co.uk

Jasmin Paris' website: www.jasminfellrunner.blogspot.co.uk

Keri Wallace's guided running company: www.girlsonhills.com

John Fleetwood's website has more route ideas than most of us can squeeze into a lifetime: www.longdistancechallenges.blogspot.co.uk

A 30-minute documentary about the Dinorwig quarry: https://www.youtube.com/watch?v=enUeHEipHt4

Books

In alphabetical order (by title), both inspiration and information:

Feet in the Clouds by Richard Askwith. Aurum Press, 2003. A benchmark piece of sports journalism.

Forbidden Land: The struggle for access to mountain and moorland by Tom Stephenson. Manchester University Press, 1989. Historical background on matters of access and recreation.

History and Records of Notable Fell Walks, 1864–1972, within the Lake District, by Fred Rogerson, self-published (out of print).

It's a hill, get over it by Steve Chilton. Sandstone Press, 2014.

Mud, Sweat and Tears: An Irish woman's journey of self-discovery, by Moire O' Sullivan. Self-published, 2011. A personal account of the first completion of the Wicklow Round (see www.moireosullivan.com).

Rhosydd Slate Quarry, by MJT Lewis and JH Denton. Shrewsbury: Cottage Press, 1974

Running Beyond: Epic ultra, trail and skyrunning races by Ian Corless. Aurum Press, 2010.

Stud Marks on the Summits: A history of amateur fell racing: 1861–1983, by Bill Smith. SKG publications, 1985 (out of print).

The Mountains are Calling by Jonny Muir. Sandstone Press, 2017.

Trail and Mountain Running by Sarah Rowell and Wendy Dodds. The Crowood Press Ltd, 2013. An excellent book on fitness, training, tactics, technique and strategies for hill running.

The Round by Steve Chilton. Sandstone Press, 2016.

Wild Trails to Far Horizons: An ultra-distance runner, by Mike Cudahy. Hayloft Publishing, 2009. This includes Mike Hartley's thrilling account of the Big Three back to back: 'Round and Round and Round'.

42 Peaks – the Story of the Bob Graham Round by Roger Smith, 3rd edition edited and updated by Paddy Buckley and Brian Covell. Hayloft Publishing, 2009 (first published 1982). Essential reading for every contender.

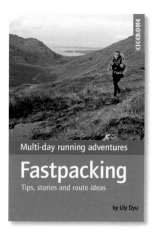
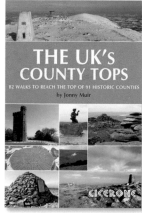
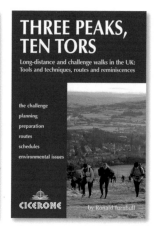
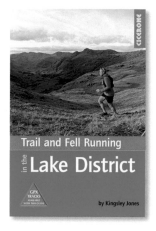
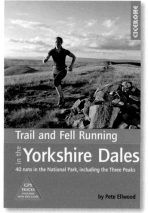
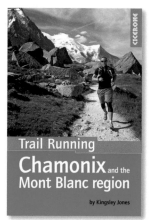

The Mamores at sunset, from Mullach nan Coirean, Charlie Ramsay Round

Listing of Cicerone Guides

Alps cross-border routes
100 Hut Walks in the Alps
Across the Eastern Alps: E5
Alpine Ski Mountaineering
  Vol 1 – Western Alps
Alpine Ski Mountaineering
  Vol 2 – Central and Eastern Alps
Chamonix to Zermatt
The Karnischer Hohenweg
The Tour of the Bernina
Tour of Mont Blanc
Tour of Monte Rosa
Tour of the Matterhorn
Trail Running – Chamonix and
  the Mont Blanc region
Trekking in the Alps
Trekking in the Silvretta
  and Rätikon Alps
Trekking Munich to Venice
Walking in the Alps

Pyrenees and France/Spain cross-border routes
The GR10 Trail
The GR11 Trail
The Pyrenean Haute Route
The Pyrenees
The Way of St James – Spain
Walks and Climbs in the Pyrenees

Austria
Innsbruck Mountain Adventures
The Adlerweg
Trekking in Austria's Hohe Tauern
Trekking in the Stubai Alps
Trekking in the Zillertal Alps
Walking in Austria

Switzerland
Cycle Touring in Switzerland
Switzerland's Jura Crest Trail
The Swiss Alpine Pass Route
  – Via Alpina Route 1
The Swiss Alps
Tour of the Jungfrau Region
Walking in the Bernese Oberland
Walking in the Valais

France and Belgium
Chamonix Mountain Adventures
Cycle Touring in France
Cycling London to Paris
Cycling the Canal de la Garonne
Cycling the Canal du Midi
Écrins National Park
Mont Blanc Walks
Mountain Adventures
  in the Maurienne
The GR20 Corsica
The GR5 Trail
The GR5 Trail – Vosges and Jura
The Grand Traverse of
  the Massif Central
The Loire Cycle Route
The Moselle Cycle Route
The River Rhone Cycle Route
The Robert Louis Stevenson Trail
The Way of St James – Le Puy
  to the Pyrenees
Tour of the Oisans: The GR54
Tour of the Queyras

Vanoise Ski Touring
Via Ferratas of the French Alps
Walking in Corsica
Walking in Provence – East
Walking in Provence – West
Walking in the Auvergne
Walking in the Briançonnais
Walking in the Cevennes
Walking in the Dordogne
Walking in the Haute
  Savoie: North
Walking in the Haute
  Savoie: South
Walks in the Cathar Region
The GR5 Trail – Benelux
  and Lorraine
Walking in the Ardennes

Germany
Hiking and Cycling in
  the Black Forest
The Danube Cycleway Vol 1
The Rhine Cycle Route
The Westweg
Walking in the Bavarian Alps

Iceland and Greenland
Trekking in Greenland –
  The Arctic Circle Trail
Walking and Trekking in Iceland

Ireland
The Irish Coast to Coast Walk
The Mountains of Ireland
The Wild Atlantic Way and
  Western Ireland

Italy
Italy's Sibillini National Park
Shorter Walks in the Dolomites
Ski Touring and Snowshoeing
  in the Dolomites
The Way of St Francis
Through the Italian Alps
Trekking in the Apennines
Trekking in the Dolomites
Via Ferratas of the Italian
  Dolomites: Vol 1
Via Ferratas of the Italian
  Dolomites: Vol 2
Walking and Trekking in
  the Gran Paradiso
Walking in Abruzzo
Walking in Italy's Stelvio
  National Park
Walking in Sardinia
Walking in Sicily
Walking in the Dolomites
Walking in Tuscany
Walking in Umbria
Walking Lake Garda and Iseo
Walking on the Amalfi Coast
Walking the Italian Lakes
Walks and Treks in the
  Maritime Alps

Scandinavia
Walking in Norway

Eastern Europe and the Balkans
The Danube Cycleway Vol 2
The High Tatras
The Mountains of Romania
Walking in Bulgaria's
  National Parks
Walking in Hungary
Mountain Biking in Slovenia
The Islands of Croatia
The Julian Alps of Slovenia
The Mountains of Montenegro
The Peaks of the Balkans Trail
The Slovenian Mountain Trail
Walking in Croatia
Walking in Slovenia:
  The Karavanke

Spain and Portugal
Coastal Walks in Andalucia
Cycle Touring in Spain
Cycling the Camino de Santiago
Mountain Walking in Mallorca
Mountain Walking in
  Southern Catalunya
Spain's Sendero Histórico:
  The GR1
The Andalucian Coast
  to Coast Walk
The Mountains of Nerja
The Mountains of Ronda
  and Grazalema
The Northern Caminos
The Sierras of Extremadura
Trekking in Mallorca
Walking and Trekking in
  the Sierra Nevada
Walking in Andalucia
Walking in Menorca
Walking in the Cordillera
  Cantabrica
Walking on Gran Canaria
Walking on La Gomera
  and El Hierro
Walking on La Palma
Walking on Lanzarote
  and Fuerteventura
Walking on Tenerife
Walking on the Costa Blanca
The Camino Portugués
Walking in Portugal
Walking in the Algarve
Walking on Madeira

Greece, Cyprus and Malta
The High Mountains of Crete
Trekking in Greece
Walking and Trekking in Zagori
Walking and Trekking on Corfu
Walking in Cyprus
Walking on Malta

International Challenges, Collections and Activities
Canyoning in the Alps
Europe's High Points
The Via Francigena
  Canterbury to Rome – Part 2

Africa
Mountaineering in the
  Moroccan High Atlas
The High Atlas
Trekking in the Atlas Mountains
Walks and Scrambles in the
  Moroccan Anti-Atlas
Kilimanjaro
Walking in the Drakensberg

Asia
Trekking in Tajikistan
Japan's Kumano Kodo Pilgrimage
Walking and Trekking in the
  Japan Alps and Mount Fuji
Jordan – Walks, Treks, Caves,
  Climbs and Canyons
Treks and Climbs in Wadi
  Rum, Jordan
Annapurna
Everest: A Trekker's Guide
Trekking in the Himalaya
Trekking in Bhutan
Trekking in Ladakh
The Mount Kailash Trek

North America
British Columbia
The John Muir Trail
The Pacific Crest Trail

South America
Aconcagua and the
  Southern Andes
Hiking and Biking Peru's Inca Trails
Torres del Paine

Techniques
Fastpacking
Geocaching in the UK
Indoor Climbing
Lightweight Camping
Map and Compass
Outdoor Photography
Polar Exploration
Rock Climbing
Sport Climbing
The Mountain Hut Book

Mini Guides
Alpine Flowers
Avalanche!
Navigation
Pocket First Aid and
  Wilderness Medicine
Snow

Mountain Literature
8000 metres
A Walk in the Clouds
Abode of the Gods
Fifty Years of Adventure
The Pennine Way – the Path,
  the People, the Journey
Unjustifiable Risk?

For full information on all our guides, books and eBooks, visit our website:
www.cicerone.co.uk

Walking – Trekking – Mountaineering – Climbing – Cycling

Over 50 years, Cicerone have built up an outstanding collection of over 300 guides, inspiring all sorts of amazing adventures.

Every guide comes from extensive exploration and research by our expert authors, all with a passion for their subjects. They are frequently praised, endorsed and used by clubs, instructors and outdoor organisations.

All our titles can now be bought as **e-books**, **ePubs** and **Kindle** files and we also have an online magazine – **Cicerone Extra** – with features to help cyclists, climbers, walkers and trekkers choose their next adventure, at home or abroad.

Our website shows any **new information** we've had in since a book was published. Please do let us know if you find anything has changed, so that we can publish the latest details. On our **website** you'll also find great ideas and lots of detailed information about what's inside every guide and you can buy **individual routes** from many of them online.

It's easy to keep in touch with what's going on at Cicerone by getting our monthly **free e-newsletter**, which is full of offers, competitions, up-to-date information and topical articles. You can subscribe on our home page and also follow us on **Facebook** and **Twitter** or dip into our **blog**.

Cicerone – the very best guides for exploring the world.

CICERONE

Juniper House, Murley Moss, Oxenholme Road, Kendal, Cumbria LA9 7RL
Tel: 015395 62069 info@cicerone.co.uk
www.cicerone.co.uk